EXMOOR WALKS FOR MOTORISTS

WALKS FOR MOTORISTS EXMOOR

David Beazley

Thirty circular walks
with sketch maps by
C. G. Edwards and D. L. Indge

EXMOOR BOOKS

First published by Frederick Warne 1979
This edition published by Exmoor Books 1990.
Revised and updated edition 1992.

Copyright © Exmoor Books 1990, 1992
ISBN: 0 086183-182-9

British Library Cataloguing-in-Publication Data

CIP Catalogue Record for this book is available from the British Library.

EXMOOR BOOKS
Official Publisher to Exmoor National Park Authority

EXMOOR BOOKS
Dulverton, Somerset

Trade sales enquiries:
Westcountry Books
Chinon Court
Lower Moor Way
Tiverton. EX16 6SS
Tel: 0884 243242
Fax: 0884 243325

*Exmoor Books is a partnership between
The Exmoor Press and Exmoor National Park*

Designed for Exmoor Books by
Topics Visual Information
397 Topsham Road
Exeter EX2 6HD
Tel: 0392 876800

Typeset by ICON, Exeter
Printed and bound in Great Britain by BPCC Wheatons Ltd, Exeter

Contents

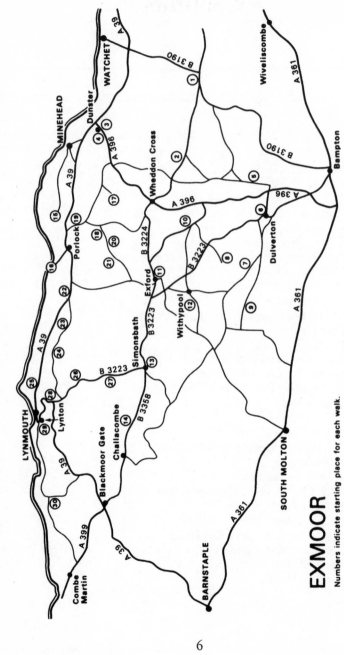

EXMOOR

Numbers indicate starting place for each walk.

6

Introduction

Although Exmoor is the second smallest of the ten National Parks in England and Wales, it is probably the most attractive area for the casual walker. There are 600 miles of rights of way over footpaths and bridleways and many thousands of acres of open moorland on which public access is permitted. The absence of spectacular heights is compensated for by the overall friendliness and intimacy of the countryside which is normally 'walkable' throughout the year. The risks in walking within Exmoor National Park are minimal and elementary care will ensure that enjoyment is not marred.

The designation of Exmoor as a National Park means that the local authority has the responsibility of ensuring that its natural beauty is conserved and that there is ample opportunity for public enjoyment of its attributes. No National Parks in this country are publicly owned and in Exmoor the large majority of its 170,000 acres are owned by the private individuals who live and work there.

Efforts by the Exmoor National Park authority to protect the interests of the landowners and ensure the enjoyment of visitors are typified by the thorough signposting and waymarking of nearly one third of the total path mileage. These are detailed in their own publications but the object of *this* walker's guide is to take present day conditions into account and provide a ready made package of pleasure for the visitors who are attracted by what they see from their car and would like to explore a little further. Public transport is now virtually non-existent, so all suggested walks are circular, starting and finishing at a recognized and legitimate car parking area.

In addition to this guide, there are a few other items of equipment which will ensure the success of the walks. Sound walking boots are a good investment because they provide proper support, warmth and most important – dry feet! However, it is feasible to walk in shoes and if the going is wet, wellington boots with a good lining of socks are recommended.

The sketch maps for each walk are adequate for confirming the overall route but the Ordnance Survey One Inch Tourist Map of Exmoor covers the whole area and is a wise buy if you are walking or motoring in the area.

To further assist in finding the starting point of each walk, a six figure map reference is given. To find the place indicated on the map, take the first three numbers of the reference and then relate them to the numbers along the top of the relevant Ordnance Survey map. For instance, if the first three numbers are 892, the reference line is two-tenths of a square east of the line marked 89 and runs downwards. Now take the second 3 numbers and relate them to the numbers running down the side of the map. If the second three numbers of the reference are 416, the reference line is six-tenths of a square north of the line marked 41 and runs across the map. Then the place indicated by the map reference 892416 is found where the two reference lines intersect. In fact, on any Ordnance Survey map of Exmoor, this map reference is the one for Dunkery Beacon, at 1705 feet the highest point on Exmoor. Always remember, the first three numbers give the 'easting' and the second three numbers the 'northing'.

There are many first class guides to trees, flowers, birds, mammals etc. and the flora and fauna of Exmoor are so diversified, it would be well worth while adding the weight of one or more of these to your burden together with a pair of binoculars. Places for refreshment, either at the starting point or en route are available on about half of the walks but as picnic meals contribute so much to a walk in the countryside, no special effort has been made to route the other walks any nearer to the well spread hostelries.

For many walkers, satisfaction is incomplete without the companionship of their dog. This is feasible on all these walks but for the dog's sake and your own peace of mind, the dog should not only be under control but be seen to be under control. Although your dog may have a long proven record of good behaviour amongst farm animals, the animals do not know this and there have been horrific instances of injury to sheep which have taken fright when dogs have merely shown curiosity.

A feature of Exmoor is the widespread use of horses for everyday work, trekking and hunting. In a period of wet weather this can have a detrimental effect on some of the footpaths and bridleways. Most of the paths which are liable to this abuse have been omitted from these walks but muddy stretches and caravans of horses can be encountered. This may well be an occasional small inconvenience but generally the advantage is on the walkers' side because the traditional access for riders means that more paths are kept open for them. Although hunting with hounds and horses is not everyone's choice of sport, it is worth considering the point of view that were it not for the carefully planned conservation methods of the Devon and Somerset Stag Hounds, the red deer would very soon be eliminated from Exmoor. On many of these walks, the sight of red deer in their natural environment can be a lasting memory.

During the course of your walks it is probable that you will meet one of the team of six professional National Park Rangers. Their duty is not law enforcement but to physically ensure the achievement of the National Park objectives: conservation and public enjoyment.

The Country Code is their criterion and if this is observed by all those who visit Exmoor, its continued existence as an area of unique beauty is ensured. Perhaps, it would be as well to finalize this introduction with a reminder of the points of this 'code of good behaviour':

Guard against all risk of fire Every year there is incalculable loss through accidental fires caused by carelessness with dropped matches and cigarette ends.

Fasten all 'gates Particular care taken in this respect will be especially appreciated by Exmoor farmers whose successful livestock and grass-land management is dependant upon these gates.

Keep dogs under proper control Already mentioned.

Keep to the paths across farmland When in doubt, walk around the field boundaries remembering that grass is the main crop in Exmoor and can be ruined by too many feet.

Avoid damaging fences, hedges and walls Repairs to these essential boundaries are an unlooked for item of farm expense which can be prevented if you keep to the gates and stiles on the rights of way.

Leave no litter Exmoor is a clean area – please keep it so and take your litter home.

Safeguard water supplies Despite the heavy annual rainfall in the centre of Exmoor, very little water is retained and of course there are no water mains for the scattered population. Please keep clear of all water collecting areas and hydraulic rams.

Protect wild life, wild plants and trees This is only achieved by observation and *not* collection.

Go carefully on country roads Exmoor roads are not suitable for speed. Please take care when you are driving and if you are walking, keep a sharp look out for those drivers who have forgotten where they are.

Respect the life of the countryside Please try to fit in with the life and work of the countryside. This will ensure a welcome for you and for those visitors who follow you.

9

Comberow and the Old Mineral Line
6½ miles (10.5 km)

OS sheet 181
Start: View point on B3190, 400 yards W. of Raleigh's Cross Inn,
OS map ref. 035343

This walk starts on the highest ridge of the Brendon Hills, dominant feature of eastern Exmoor. From the start point there is a breathtaking view to the north with woodlands clothing the deep combes and rounded hills and a patchwork of fields stretching from the foothills to the red soil of the coastal strip. In the background is the Bristol Channel and beyond this, on a clear day, the South Wales coast and Brecon Beacons can be seen.

Mining for iron ore has been carried on in the Brendons since at least Elizabethan times and extensive working took place from the middle of the 19th century. After a chequered existence, this industry ceased at the turn of the century with a brief re-opening from 1907 to 1910. A railway line was specially constructed to link up the mines along the ridge with Watchet harbour 1300 feet below and this walk crosses the remarkable incline, ¾ mile long with a gradient of 1 in 4, which was built from Comberow to the summit 800 feet above.

Inevitably there are steep hills to be descended and climbed again on this walk and some stretches can be muddy but stout shoes can cope with this, except during a spell of very wet weather, when boots are recommended.

To reach the start point take the B3190 south from Washford Cross on the A39 or north from Bampton. If there is insufficient space for car parking at the view point there are suitable wide verges near at hand.

Walk westwards (towards Bampton) along the road for 400 yards, taking great care because this is one of the very rare stretches of straight road on Exmoor and frustrated motorists are apt to drive very fast along it. Turn right off the road where there is a footpath sign to Roadwater via Comberow. As far as Comberow there will be red waymarks to confirm the route to be followed. The path starts as a wide grassy track between two fields, then goes through a gate into a spruce plantation. Carry on downhill, curving slightly left and at the end of the plantation turn left to walk uphill for 30 yards, then turn right through a hedge and follow the track down into a small combe, across the stream and up the other side. The path descends again to cross another stream and then

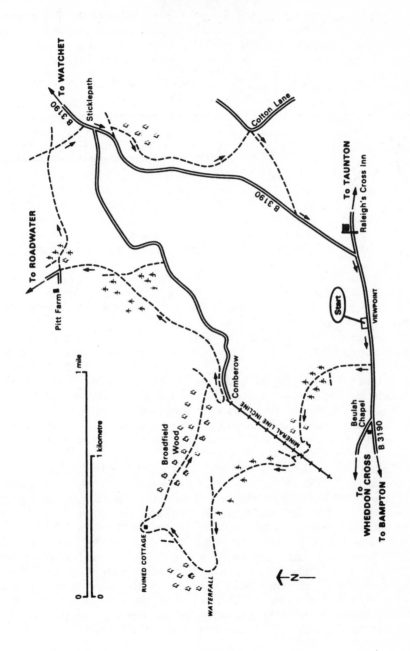

cuts into the incline section of the old mineral railway line. This is now sadly overgrown but the immense task involved in blasting this section out of the rock can be readily appreciated. At the top of the incline was the winding house where the hauling machinery was housed and the remains of this building can still be seen on the right hand side of the road to Wheddon Cross, just after Beulah Chapel.

Walk straight across the incline, turn right and climb again, turning left at a T-junction 50 yards from the incline. Now the path passes through forestry plantations again. Turn right to walk under a hedge to the left until a hunting gate is reached. From this point the path descends progressively more steeply until it joins a track running from right to left. Turn left here by the signpost and carry on downhill until the path veers left and steeply uphill just beyond a small clearing to the right. This is a dramatic spot with the very steep tree clad hills all around and the noise of cascading water in front. Very soon the water-fall is reached where the water plunges 50 feet down the sheer rock face and is then culverted under the path. Follow the track round to the right.

The next stretch is frequently muddy, and after passing cypress trees and Douglas firs on the right, take the right fork and then turn left to skirt around a wild combe. After crossing a stream there is a ruined cot-tage on the right, (too isolated for a holiday home!), and the path divides again. Take the right fork signposted to Comberow and now the path passes through overgrown woodland with a wide variety of hard-wood trees. Because of the age of these trees, some difficulty has been encountered in keeping the path clear. It follows the line of the stream which was crossed just before the cottage and climbs a little as the houses of Comberow come into sight over to the right. Turn sharp right as the path narrows and descend to cross the stream. This is where the Mineral Line incline started. The station itself has been demolished but the stationmaster's house still exists.

Take the first turning on the left after crossing the bridge, signposted 'Roadwater 2', and for the next mile it is a level walk along the actual course of the old railway line. Ignore the red waymark signs on a path crossing the line and pass a picture postcard cottage on the left with immaculate gardens set each side of the stream. The next building on the left is Pitt farm. Turn sharp right here opposite the farm entrance and climb up through a plantation of mixed conifers and hardwoods on a zigzag path until another yellow waymarked path is reached. Turn right onto this path which goes to a gate on the wood boundary. Go straight through the gate and carry on along the edge of a field with a valley below to the right and steep hillside beyond. The path climbs steadily along until a field gate is reached which opens from a lane.

Turn right into the lane – do not follow the yellow waymarks any further – and follow it to the B3190 road. To the left beyond Chidgley Farm, there is a fine view of the Quantock Hills.

Turn right up the road for 250 yards and then turn left onto a track signposted to Monksilver and Raleigh's Cross. 150 yards past the cottage on the right, the path forks. Turn sharp right here and from this point there are red waymarks again to confirm the line of the path. There is a steady climb now with plenty of opportunities to enjoy the panoramic scenes to the right. After passing through woodlands go through a gate, veering left to keep parallel with the wood boundary. At the end of the wood go straight through the next gate and follow the line of a beech hedge, which veers right at the top of the field, to the next gate. Pass through this gate and again follow the line of the hedge to the left. Go through a gate at the end of this field into a road (Colton Lane). Turn half right here and go through the gate to the left of a wire fence. There is a signpost here for Raleigh's Cross and the correct gate is to left of this. Follow the fence closely to the gate into the next field, go through this gate and incline left to follow the hedge boundary on the left to the B3190 road again. Turn left onto the road and follow it back to the car, passing Raleigh's Cross Inn on the left and the auction field where many thousands of locally bred sheep are sold at sales in late summer and autumn.

Kennisham, Colly and Lype Hills
4 miles (6.5 km)

OS sheet 181
Start: Entrance to Kennisham Hill Wood at Goosemoor on the Wheddon
Cross to Raleigh's Cross road, OS map ref. 964358

This is another walk in the Brendon Hills which takes a route through forestry plantations and across pastures, some of which have only been improved from rough grazing in recent years. In the latter part of the walk on Colly and Lype Hills, please take care to follow the route and walk around and not across fields. Lype Hill at the western extremity of this walk is the highest point in the Brendon Hills at nearly 1400 feet. Kennisham woods were seriously damaged in the severe gales of January 1976 and January 1990 and evidence of this battering can still be seen. However, much of the debris has now been removed and the replacement trees are now growing strongly.

There are no very steep gradients on this walk but there may be a damp stretch in the lower part of the woodland. It is most important to keep dogs under control because in addition to sheep, large numbers of pheasants are bred in this area.

The starting point is 3 miles from Wheddon Cross at a junction with a road from Brompton Regis. Wheddon Cross is reached on the A396 from Dunster or Tiverton, or on the B3224 from Exford. Cars can be parked in the new picnic site and viewing area just inside the woods on the right. This has been provided by the Forestry Commission to replace another site farther east which is now masked by the rapid growth of surrounding conifers.

Start off along the forestry track, running northeastwards from the picnic site. In front will be seen Croydon hill with the largest Forestry Commission woods in the area. Keep straight on at the intersection with other forestry tracks from left and right. At this point, looking half left there is a glimpse of the Bristol Channel with the mountains of Wales beyond.

Carry on downhill to the edge of the wood and go through the gate immediately in front. Walk by the side of the hedge on the right until the hedge turns right, then turn half left to a gate leading into a woodland track with a steep valley on the left. Go through this gate and follow the track which shortly joins a forestry road. After about 600 yards turn left downhill on this road at a junction with other tracks.

14

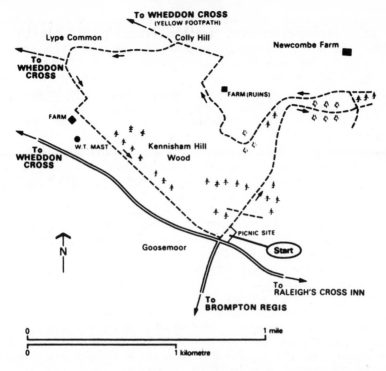

To **WHEDDON CROSS**
(YELLOW FOOTPATH)

Lype Common   Colly Hill

Newcombe Farm

To
WHEDDON
CROSS

FARM (RUINS)

FARM

W.T. MAST   Kennisham Hill
Wood

To
WHEDDON
CROSS

N

Goosemoor   PICNIC SITE

Start

To
RALEIGH'S CROSS INN

To
BROMPTON REGIS

0   1 mile

0   1 kilometre

Opposite Newcombe Farm this runs into another wide forestry road. Turn left onto this road and from here onwards follow red waymarks, climbing gradually alongside pheasant rearing pens with a brook down to right.

After the pens, the path passes through some predominately beech woods to a gate into a meadow. Go straight through and walk along the boundary of the meadow and wood. At the far end go through another gate and alongside the stream for 20 yards, cross the stream and follow the marked path up through a tangle of trees. The red waymarked path follows a sunken track steeply upwards to a gate out of the wood. Go through the gate and follow the fence on the right to the top of the field which has a solitary tree and a ruined building on the left. Turn right, and now is a good time to take a breather. Looking back across the valley, the course of the path through Kennisham Wood can be traced, and looking ahead there are the Quantock Hills with the Mendip Hills beyond in the far distance.

Follow the red waymarked path along the left hand side of the hedge, turning left after about 300 yards to follow a wire fence, with ruined

15

farm buildings down below to the right. These ruins are a symptom of the depopulation in the area. One hundred years ago the land supported a far greater number of families, but changed farming methods now need less labour and there are no alternative forms of employment. Locally, in the Brendons, this trend has been accentuated by the abandonment of mining which provided employment for many hundreds of men when production was at its peak.

At the top of this field, go through the gate in front and then turn right along a hedge. At the corner of the field turn left to follow path signposted to Wheddon Cross and walk along the boundary of the same field until a wire fence is reached. Turn left again here and after 40 yards there is a three-way footpath sign at the path junction on Colly Hill.

Continue to follow the red waymarked path towards Wheddon Cross and go through the gate adjacent to the sign. Follow the same wire fence, turning half right as the fence divides. To the left is the very conspicuous landmark of the W.T. mast at the western end of Kennisham Wood. This mast is a useful landmark because it can be seen from very many points in the eastern half of Exmoor. Go through the second gate on the left and carry on in the same direction on the other side of the fence up to the corner of the field and then turn left to the next gateway. In front is the renowned view point at Lype Hill with fine views of Dunkery Beacon and the Aville valley leading down to Dunster. It is also usually very windy and if there is a nip in the air, your progress onto the last stage of the walk will be accelerated.

At this point leave the red waymarked path which carries on to Wheddon Cross. Go through the gate then turn left to follow the fence leading towards Kennisham Wood. Turn right at the corner of the field and then turn left through the first gate on the left. Cross a small field with farm buildings on the right to a gate leading into the wood. Go through the gate and keep straight on to take a wide forestry road running south-southeast back to the start point.

Dunster Park
3¹/₄ miles (5 km)

OS sheet 181
Start: Car park adjacent to Gallox Bridge, Dunster, OS map ref. 990433

Dunster is probably the busiest village in modern day Exmoor and it can be a relief to set off on one of the many footpaths radiating from its centre, thus escaping the conflict of history and commerce. The ancient buildings have withstood the intrusion remarkably well. The Yarn Market standing in the main street and proclaiming the importance of Dunster as a trading centre for wool was built in 1609 and, although damaged in 1646 during the 6 month siege of the castle in the Civil War, still withstands the pressures of intense motor traffic.

Near at hand the Luttrell Arms Hotel was built in the 16th century and commemorates the long association which the Luttrell family have had with Dunster. They purchased Dunster Castle from the Norman family of de Mohuns in 1376 and retained it until 1976 when Col. Luttrell presented it to the National Trust together with 30 acres of parkland. The original castle was built in 1070 on the site of an old Saxon fortress, but none of this stands today. Most of the present building was completed in the 16th and 17th centuries although the inner gatehouse is thought to date back to the 13th century. The Deer Park over which this walk takes place was enclosed by Henry Fownes Luttrell between 1755 and 1758 and many of the fine trees still standing in the park were planted by the same man.

A visit to the Exmoor National Park Visitor Centre near the main car park on Dunster Steep is a "must" on your first visit to Dunster. To reach the start point, turn off the A396 as it enters Dunster from the Timberscombe direction, down Park St adjacent to the Foresters Arms. The car park is at the bottom on the left hand side.

Turn left out of the car park and pass the children's playground on the right with its protection of lofty poplars. Until recently these trees were complemented by sturdy elms, but these had to be removed as a result of Dutch elm disease. Cross the Gallox Bridge over the River Avill. The bridge is so named because it is the route to Gallox Hill where the public gallows once stood. Pass the thatched cottages on the right, bear left to Park Gate and climb over the stile. A sign indicates the public path to Withycombe on the right and this is the path on which to start. On this stage there are red waymarks to confirm the route. At the next

17

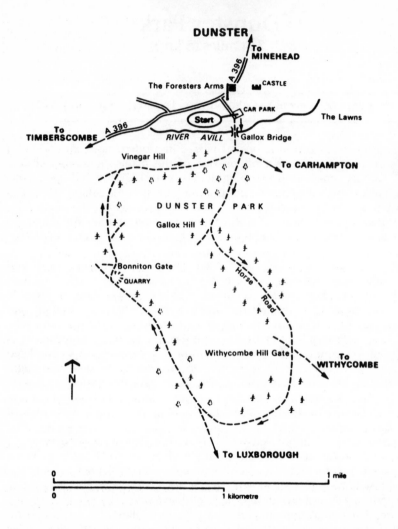

gate look back for a fine view of Dunster Castle with the Lawns to the right. In the early part of the century this was the site of one of the finest polo grounds in the country.

As the path now climbs steadily uphill with a small stream on the right, Gallox Hill is the one up above to the right. Keep to the main path along the side of the stream and notice the young trees which are progressing well towards replacing the venerable oaks on each side. The stream vanishes and after some bracken covered slopes there is a conifer plantation on the right, mainly comprising spruce and larch with the native silver birch holding its own here and there. When the path divides, take the left fork and proceed up Horse Road. As will be seen, this is well named because there is ample evidence that many riders use all these paths in Dunster Park.

The next landmark is a massive V shaped oak on the left. Keep to the main track which is adequately indicated by the red waymarks.

Climb steadily and a stone faced bank on the left will indicate the end of this climb. Opposite the footpath sign to Withycombe, turn left to go through Withycombe Hill Gate and then turn immediately right to leave the red waymarked path and follow a vehicle track which runs parallel with the boundary bank on the right. As the path descends, the prominent feature in front is Black Hill. Still going downhill this track sweeps round to the right with woodland on both sides and a drop on the left to a stream. There are some very fine specimen trees, both conifers and hardwoods, along this sheltered valley and a profusion of wild flowers along the banks of the stream which is reached when the track joins another woodland road.

Keep straight on from this junction, and from here the route back to Gallox Bridge is confirmed by blue waymarks. There is a gentle easy stroll now, keeping the babbling stream on the left. On the right there are some small quarries from which the stone for forest roads has been extracted. In the second of these quarries fork off to the right and climb uphill on a forest road which has a variety of conifers on both sides. After a steady pull uphill, the road turns sharp right and then descends to another junction. Keep straight on passing Bonniton Gate on the right and aiming for some splendid pine trees in front. From the middle of these pine trees, Grabbist Hill appears in front on the other side of the valley and it is surprising to note how much height has been gained since forking off at the quarry.

As the path starts to descend, fork left. Just after this fork it is well worth making a diversion to the small promontory in a clearing on the left. The view from here, especially in the direction of Dunkery Beacon is a just reward for the effort.

It is a steady descent from Vinegar Hill now with dense banks of rhododendrons below to the left. All along this section of path there are remarkable examples of a wide variety of trees, many of them planted 200 years ago. Amongst some cedars the path is joined by a yellow way-marked path and shortly after this junction the outskirts of Dunster can be glimpsed down to the left. Very soon the path returns to Gallox Bridge after covering one of the most varied woodland walks that Exmoor can offer.

Dunster around Grabbist Hill
4½ miles (7 km)

OS sheet 181
Start: Frackford Bridge, Dunster, OS map ref. 985433

O n the previous walk, Dunster Park, which lies to the south of Dunster was explored; on this walk Grabbist Hill which overlooks Dunster from the west is climbed – as gently as possible! The walk also goes through majestic mature woodland above Alcombe and passes a sad reminder of the havoc caused by fire in the arid summer of 1976. Very early in that summer, fires ravaged a large part of the forestry plantation in this area and it was only the herculean efforts of local fire brigades assisted by volunteers that prevented much greater damage. Lessons learnt from this outbreak early in that summer stood Exmoor in good stead because there were no further tragedies of this size in that year. This particular fire was thought to have been started by magnification of the sun's rays on a broken bottle.

The starting point for this walk is on the A396 road from Dunster, 350 yards beyond the Foresters Arms and just before Frackford Bridge over the river Avill. On the right hand side of the road travelling towards Timberscombe there is a wide turning which is not signposted. Immediately after turning into this road, there is parking space on the left.

To start the walk, take the bridleway running up into the wood on the opposite side of the road. This path runs parallel with the Dunster road, climbing steadily past a recently cleared area on the right and oak trees on the left. As it reaches a point opposite the first houses of Dunster, the path veers left and then joins another path. Turn left onto this path and for the next section the route is yellow waymarked. Now there is an easy climb through Grabbist Coppice with a steep gradient down to the left into the Avill valley. *Avill* was the Saxon word for apple and this low lying valley is probably the only area in Exmoor where it is possible to cultivate this fruit.

From the first seat along this path, there are views of Dunster Park to the left, with bare Black Hill beyond, and in front can be seen the extensive Forestry Commission plantations on Croydon Hill. Not long after this seat, the path ascends more steeply and there is a small plantation of beech and larch on the left. Soon there is open hillside on the

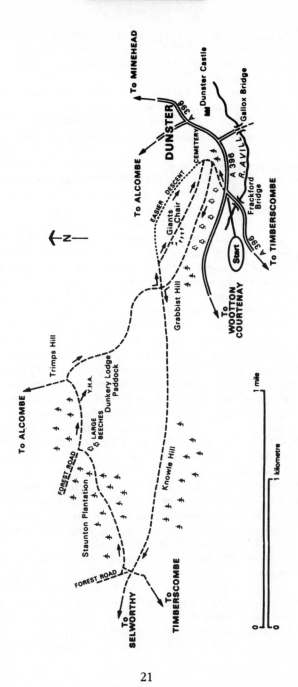

right and then, by another strategically placed seat, there is suddenly a panoramic view of most of Minehead with North Hill on the left, the harbour under the hill, Somerwest World in front and the golf course running alongside the sea to the right.

Turn left immediately after the seat onto the wide track, going slightly uphill and still following the yellow waymarks. It is open walking here past a long stretch of fire damaged woodland on the left. There are fine views to all points of the compass, especially east towards the Quantock Hills and north to Wales. Keeping on the wide track, the next landmark is the gate leading into the undamaged plantation on Knowle Hill. Do not go through the gate but take the path to the right of the boundary of this plantation. Now looking half right, nearly at the far end of North Hill can be seen the high point of Selworthy Beacon.

For a stretch there is open hillside on the right, then after going through a gap in a bank there is woodland on both sides, still with the beech topped boundary wall on the left. For a few hundred yards, there is a possibility of encountering mud, for the first time on this walk. Just before the path climbs again to Hopcott Common there is a prominent junction with a signpost. Turn right towards Minehead, leaving the yellow waymarked path to make its way to Selworthy and following blue waymarks instead. Do not follow the wide forestry road but take the narrower one slightly to the right and veering even further right downhill between pine trees, with graceful birches and occasional beeches forming a curtain on the left between path and pine plantations.

The going is easy now with occasional glimpses of the sea in front. As the path descends more steeply, larger pines are passed and then there are plantations of young spruce and larch. Numerous tracks and paths come in from right and left but the route to follow still carries on down-hill, indicated by blue waymarks. Near the bottom of this descent, the path turns left by a large beech tree which has been scarred by the attention of previous passers by.

200 yards further on, after crossing a small stream, the path runs into a forestry road. Turn right onto this road and follow alongside the stream until a memorial seat is reached on the left. Cross the stream here and continue on down the road in the same direction, passing the entrance to Minehead Youth Hostel on the right.

About 400 yards after the hostel entrance, turn sharply right to follow the path signposted to Dunster. Now there are red waymarks to confirm the route. On the left is gorse covered Trimps Hill which is a blaze of yellow for a considerable part of the year. For a time it is a steady stony climb up the path, then there is a level sandy stretch with Dunkery Lodge Paddock on the right. Turn right after this paddock and climb up onto the open, bracken covered hillside, turning left as instructed by the footpath sign. At first this section shows sign of heavy usage by horses but any bad patches are avoidable by diverting to the right. Again in this area there is a fire hazard which is confirmed by the spectral appearance of the dead gorse.

Fork right, away from the field boundary on the left and about 400 yards further on there is a sign confirming the direction to Dunster – straight on. More steady climbing here, bearing right when there is a choice, and then the path follows a wire fence between grassland and the open common. Turn left to follow this fence and 30 yards later a familiar spot will be encountered – the seat from which the first view of Minehead was obtained after climbing through Grabbist Coppice. Now take the left hand path marked red following the same field boundary. Fork right just after a wooden bench on the right.

If it is wished to avoid the very steep descent, fork left at this point and follow the red waymarks on a steady descent through woodland to rejoin the original route by the cemetery.

To the right is a natural plateau known as the Giant's Chair and the views from this ridge are even more spectacular with no trees in the foreground to break them up. Away to the right is Dunkery, to the left is the Conygar Tower which was built as a 'folly' by Henry Fownes Luttrell in the 18th century and away in front is Bridgewater Bay with the conspicuous hulk of Hinkley Point power station. Keep straight on and descend rapidly over grass and loose stone. Although this descent is very steep, it is rarely treacherous and should present no problem if made with care. At the bottom with the cemetery immediately in front, turn right and at the end of the wooden fence fork right. 25 yards further on fork left onto the path which leads back to the start point.

Pixton Estate and Lower Haddeo Valley

5 or 2½ miles (8 or 4 km)

OS sheet 181
Start: Louisa Gate, OS map ref. 937287 or
Bury Village, OS map ref. 945275

Alternative starting points are suggested for this walk because although Bury is the better starting place with an uphill start and level finish, car parking can be difficult, whereas space can always be found on the wide grass verges adjacent to Louisa Gate. The name of this gate has been romantically converted in recent years from its original name of Lousy Gate. A 'louse' was a pigsty or enclosure and here stood the enclosure gate at the top of Swinescleeve where the pigs spent their days searching for acorns and beechmast. Ideally, if there are two cars with the walking party, one could be left at Bury and the other used for transport to Louisa Gate because the mile between these two points includes an arduous climb with little reward in the way of scenery. However if this is not possible, the rest of the walk compensates for the effort.

To find Bury village, take the B3222 out of Dulverton (signposted Minehead) and turn right when the A396 is reached. One mile after joining this road turn left onto the minor road signposted to Watchet. Bury is just another mile along this road where it turns sharp left and then right. There may be parking space by the telephone kiosk or near the ford. To get to Louisa Gate, take the same road out of Dulverton, turn right onto the A396 and then immediately left onto the Brompton Regis road. One mile up this road, the entrance to Baronsdown Farm is on the left and the gateway immediately opposite is the Louisa Gate into the Pixton Estate.

If you have parked at Bury, walk across the footbridge over the Haddeo and keep to the right passing Cowlings and Hunts Farm up to the Hartford Drive entrance to the Pixton Estate, then turn left to follow a yellow waymarked track to Louisa Gate. This starts as a steep climb up a sunken muddy track but after 10-15 minutes a gate is reached. Go through this gate and the ascent is more gradual with fields to the left and the woods of Swinescleeve to the right. As the path levels out with

24

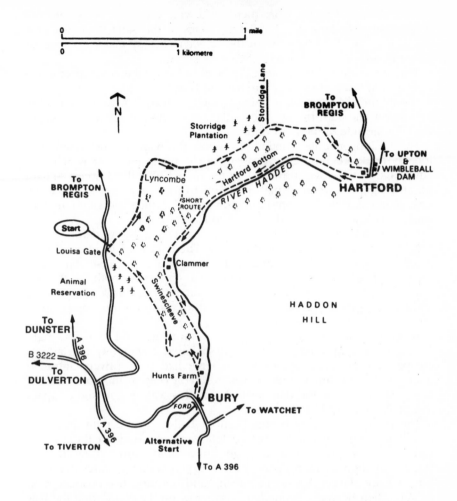

a conifer plantation on the left, Louisa Gate is reached. This is the start for those who have chosen the alternative parking place.

At Louisa Gate there is a signpost with one finger pointing left to Hartford and Upton. Follow this yellow waymarked path all the way to Hartford. Extensive forestry work has been carried out in this area over the past few years and there are many forestry tracks crossing and joining your route. When in doubt, look for and follow the waymarks. After 120 yards downhill climb over a stile, then turn left onto the wide forestry track which follows the contours through Lyncombe wood to

Storridge wood. In all seasons there are a wide variety of birds here and it is possible to hear many different songs at the same time with the occasional cry of a pheasant, or the screech of a jay making a raucous background.

Where the track skirts around the head of Lyncombe, a signpost is stationed to indicate the short route back to Bury.

If only the shorter walk is being tackled, turn right here towards Bury and follow the path by the side of the stream until it rejoins the longer walk by the side of the river Haddeo.

For the longer route, continue to follow the wide yellow waymarked forestry track, keeping an eye open for the many red deer which take advantage of the cover provided by the mixed woodland. Keep straight on at a signpost where a path forks off to Brompton Regis and at the next signpost, fork right onto a narrower track which leads into another sunken path which descends sharply to Hartford.

On the left there will be glimpses of the massive dam for the Wimbleball reservoir completed in 1979. The dam itself is tinted pink to match the local sandstone and is 161 feet high. The reservoir has a capacity of 4250 million gallons and provides water for both the Wessex and South West Water Plcs. There is a water surface area of 370 acres and many types of recreation are catered for, both on the water and in the beautiful surrounding area.

When the road is reached at Hartford, turn right and then fork right on the path signposted to Bury. The sheltered community of Hartford comprises only three houses which have had their privacy intruded upon by the construction of the vast reservoir only ½ mile upstream. If it is wished to view the dam itself during this walk follow the footpath to Upton for about ½ mile.

The route on to Bury passes Hartford Lodge on the right and trout breeding ponds on the left before following the Haddeo River along Lady Harriet's Drive. This carriage drive which runs alongside the Haddeo all the way from Pixton Park to Upton commemorates the heroism of Lady Harriet Acland in nursing and rescuing her husband Col. Acland when he was a wounded prisoner of the French during the war in America. The level of the picturesque River Haddeo is now governed by the control at the dam, but it is still the home of considerable numbers of brown trout and the occasional salmon and sea trout. There is no need for directions along this drive and for a mile or more there are no signs of human habitation.

A stream is forded and then the path is rejoined by the shorter route which followed this stream down Lyncombe. A little further on there is a very decrepit bridge across the Haddeo which it is just as well we don't have to use! Then the path passes two houses at Clammer, real 'away from it all' dwellings. Now the valley opens up and there are lush green fields below on the left. The river meanders through these fields and yet another precarious footbridge is passed. Eventually the path veers away to the right and passes through a gate by the lodge.

Immediately after the gate, turn left and retrace your steps to the car, if you started from Bury. Otherwise turn right and follow the track described in the first paragraph of the route description on p.24 until you come to Louisa Gate and the car.

Barle Valley and Court Down
3½ miles (5.5 km)

OS sheet 181
Start: Car park at Exmoor House, Dulverton, OS map ref. 913279

This walk starts at a point where the river Barle has blossomed out into a fully fledged river rushing through Dulverton before it joins the river Exe two miles further south. Dulverton itself is a thriving community which acts as a link between the southern half of Exmoor and the larger towns of Tiverton in Devon and Taunton in Somerset. As can be seen from the map, roads of various sizes fan out in all directions from the town and its narrow streets are scenes of great activity at weekends and during the holiday season. It is as well not to bank on hurrying through Dulverton at any time. There are a wide range of shops in the town, which is also well blessed with hotels and a Caravan Club site on the banks of the river. If there is time to spare, it is well worth visiting the Exmoor National Park Information Centre which is adjacent to the car park where the walk starts. This provides an excellent opportunity for learning about life in Dulverton and the surrounding area.

To commence this walk, return to the Bridge Inn and turn right over the bridge. Turn right again along a road which is the start of paths to Hawkridge and Tarr Steps. Carry straight on up this road passing Rose Cottage and The Mount on the left, then a short steep climb amongst the fragrance of wild garlic to a signpost by the thatched cottage. Continue straight ahead and in a few yards, a gap in the hedge will give a good view of the older part of Dulverton huddled below the church and the school. The path now enters Burridge Wood which was purchased for public enjoyment through the generosity of Miss B. K. Abbott and Mr. Auberon Herbert, late of Dulverton and Pixton respectively. On the left of the path is a memorial plaque to mark these gifts.

It is possible to climb up to the top of this wood to Oldberry Castle, one of the many Iron Age hill forts to be found on Exmoor. Now there are only earth banks to mark the site but it is still possible to appreciate the strategic siting of this fort before trees masked the views. On the way up through the woods there is a very good chance of sighting some of the red deer which seem to use this area for cover and feeding nearly all the year round. Here again the flourishing rhododendrons are choking the trees but efforts are being made to control them by the National Park authority. On

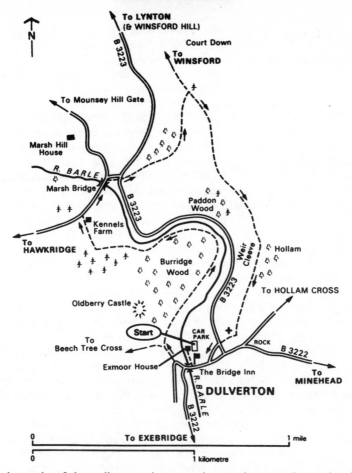

the other side of the valley can be seen the nearly vertical woods of Weir Cleeve. These are also managed by the National Park. So the future of this scenic entrance to Dulverton is very much in their hands.

After passing meadows on the right, the path runs along the river bank and then climbs sharply. This is only a short climb and the path descends to river level again. As the river veers away right the path carries straight on, crossing a small stream as it leaves Burridge Wood and then there are conifers on the left, mostly spruce and larch. In front is Kennels Farm and the path passes through the farmyard to the road.

Turn right onto the road and 250 yards further on is Marsh Bridge. Just before crossing the bridge there are some grass covered ruins on the right. These are the remains of a chapel-of-ease erected by Mr. Locke of Northmoor in the late 19th century but already nearly disappeared. After crossing the recently rebuilt Marsh Bridge, turn right and cross over the small footbridge spanning a stream which joins the Barle at this point. Take the left of the two roads in front and after climbing 30 yards cross straight over the next road, using great care because there is poor visibility for motorists coming down from Winsford Hill on the left.

Now there is a stony track to follow uphill to the highest point of the walk. No directions are necessary, just keep plodding on uphill but do take time to note the remarkable mixture of trees, especially the sweet chestnuts which are comparatively rare in this area. This mixture of trees and vegetation means that there are a wide variety of birds to be spotted and both rabbits and squirrels are plentiful. It is also interesting to note the painstaking labour which went into the construction of the stone faced bank on the left. Unfortunately, deer are now playing havoc with this and neither time nor expertise is available for repairs.

At the top of the track turn sharp right onto a wide level track and immediately on the left there is a seat underneath large pine trees. Carry on southwards back towards Dulverton. Very soon there are wonderful views to the right into the Barle valley and beyond. Down to the right is Marsh Hill House overlooking the bridge crossed earlier, and to the left of this can be seen the wooded banks of the Barle wending their way back to Castle Bridge, Hawkridge and Tarr Steps. In front of you is Northmoor with conifer plantations to its left and then further left is Burridge Wood. In the distance to the right are Anstey Commons stretching up to the ridgeway which runs from Dulverton to Barnstaple. Away to the left the distant views are all in mid-Devon and on a day of good visibility the last range of hills before the coast east of Exeter can be seen.

The path descends steadily now, first through fertile farmland, then parkland on the left and the dense woods of Paddon and Weir Cleeve on the right. Further on, where the woods of Hollam run on the left, a beautiful carpet of bluebells is to be seen in the late spring. After a muddy patch, the path rises slightly and then descends sharply with banks on both sides and the centre of Dulverton unfolds in front.

Turn left on reaching the school entrance, (what a wonderful setting in which to start school life!) and, looking over the wall into the church graveyard, there can be seen the stump of what has been an unusual tree. This was in fact a 300 year old sycamore which had to be felled in 1973. Turn right down the steps leading past All Saints church and after the church gates the busy town is entered past the Bank and the Lion Hotel. The way back to the Bridge Inn is straight on down the street passing the town hall with its double flight of steps. These two hostelries together with one other are the only survivors of the twenty or more which existed 100 years ago.

Dane's Brook to Castle Bridge
3½ miles (5.5 km)

OS sheet 181
Start: Whiterocks Down, OS map ref. 870291

Two principal features of the southern part of Exmoor are the rivers Exe and Barle which rise within 2 miles of each other on the Chains, a high wet area south of Lynton. They run on parallel courses, first eastwards then south to join below Dulverton. They are short rivers but in this country of high rainfall, varying from 80 inches per year on the Chains to 60 inches at Dulverton, they gather strength very quickly.

On this walk the largest tributary of the Barle will be followed for its last dash through woodlands. This is the Dane's Brook which starts its life as Litton Water and for its whole length of eight miles constitutes the border between Devon and Somerset. There is an excellent chance of seeing red deer at most times of the year and herds of twenty or more are quite common.

To find the start point from Withypool, take the Hawkridge road and after 2½ miles fork left at the first road junction. Ignore the turnings off to the left for Tarr Steps and Hawkridge but carry straight on towards Dulverton. After nearly 5 miles from Withypool, Venford Farm will be passed on the right and 500 yards further on there is a yellow-tipped footpath sign on the right, pointing left to Hawkridge and other places. This is the walk start point and there is plenty of parking space on the roadside. Alternatively this point can be reached by taking the Hawkridge road from Dulverton, turning right at Five Cross Ways, and from this junction it is only ¾ mile to the start.

The whole of this walk is confirmed by yellow waymarks. Go through the gate and turn right to cross the first field in which can be seen some of the outcrops of white stone which give the area its name of Whiterocks Down. Go through the next gate and then be careful to take the path ¼ left *through* the gorse. There should be marker posts here to clarify the route which descends gradually to pass through a gap in a beech hedge 300 yards further on.

Carry straight on, still downhill on a well defined track, forking left 30 yards from the hedge gap. Down to the left can be heard the rush of a stream running down from Venford to the Dane's Brook. After bracken covered slopes, the path enters oak woodland and the descent steepens

31

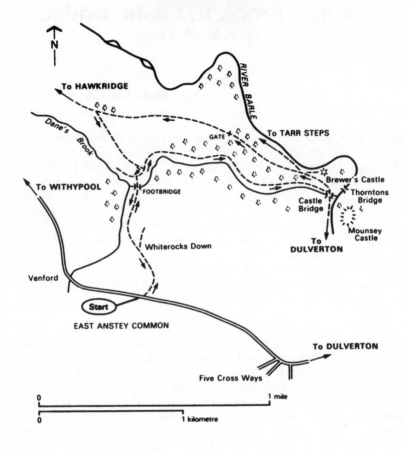

to the footbridge over the Dane's Brook. This bridge is a contribution to the comfort of Exmoor walkers by the Army. Its predecessor was completely built by Army engineers and then replacement and repairs were carried out in 1978 with the assistance of helicopters of the Army Air Corps.

Cross the bridge and carry straight on for about 25 yards. Fork right onto a wide track which climbs over a stony stretch to a three-way signpost. Continue straight on for Castle Bridge and quite soon, up to the left, it is possible to see some of the damage caused by the Winter 1990 storms. The path now follows the river and, if a closer view is required, it is possible to walk along the bank in most places instead of sticking to the path. In flood, it is an impressive sight and its flood level can be

32

appreciated by the debris left on the banks. Large dams of fallen timber are frequent because the woods on both sides are ageing. However, it will be noticed that there is plenty of natural regeneration in this woodland.

A few minutes before reaching Castle Bridge, there is a small area of National Park owned woodland where replanting of broad leaved trees has taken place. Castle Bridge crosses the river just before it enters the Barle. It gets its name from Mounsey Castle on the other side of the Barle and Brewer's Castle which lies off to the right of the next path to be taken. Although the 'castles' are named after Norman lords, they were in fact stone ramparted forts constructed for defence in the Iron Age, nearly 2500 years ago. The iron and wood bridge known as Thorntons which can be seen just upstream across the Barle belongs to the Devon and Somerset Stag Hounds and is used to facilitate hunting when the river level is too high to ford.

To continue the walk, follow the sign pointing to Tarr Steps and Hawkridge. Climb steadily uphill on a wide stony track on which Land Rovers can occasionally be encountered during the hunting season. Just before reaching the turn off to Tarr Steps, the path leading sharply back up to the right is the way to visit Brewer's Castle. Continue straight on upwards towards Hawkridge. Along here there is an impressive view of the Barle down below to the right.

The track leaves the woodland through a gate into the open grassland of Hawkridge Ridge. Follow the vehicle tracks up onto the ridge and head westward towards a row of trees at the far end of this open ground. Away to the left can be seen the starting point of this walk beside East Anstey Common and behind is the Barle valley with the tree covered Mounsey Castle prominent on the left. Go through a gate to get onto a vehicle track running to the right of the hedge containing the row of trees. To the right is another view of Barle valley where it bends sharply downstream from Tarr Steps beside the Hawkridge road.

Go past the large trees and at the end of the hedge go through the left hand gate. Turn left to follow the path signposted to East Anstey Common, rejoining the outward route at the signpost just after the 'Army' bridge across the Dane's Brook. When picking a way down this path, pause for a moment to look at the wooded valleys to the left and right which mark the course of this river. From the signpost it is just a matter of retracing the first part of the walk across the bridge and up onto Whiterocks Down with the assistance of yellow waymarks to refresh the memory.

Tarr Steps to Anstey Gate and Hawkridge

7½ or 2½ miles (12 or 4 km)

OS sheet 181
Start: Tarr Steps car park, OS map ref. 873324

The longer of these walks from Tarr Steps covers nearly the whole mixture of landscape which makes the beauty and attraction of Exmoor. In fact there is only coastal scenery missing, because there are large and small river valleys, hardwoods and conifer plantations, cultivated farmland, rough grazing and open moorland to be traversed during the course of this walk.

To reach Tarr Steps take the Exford-Dulverton road to Winsford Hill and follow the road signs from there, passing through Liscombe before turning into the large car park.

Walk down the road or the permissive scenic path to Tarr Steps, passing farm buildings and Tarr Farm on the right. Cross the clapper bridge which has spanned the Barle river for at least 700 years. Fork right up the entrance road to the hotel, which was originally Hawkridge rectory. 100 yards up this road, fork right onto a steep stony track. Go through a gate and then there is a sunken stretch up to the field corner, turn left here and follow the hedge boundary to the next gate. Pause for breath here and look back for grand views of Ashway side and the summit of Winsford Hill.

Go through the gate and walk beside the hedge on the left, through the next gate and on to another. Ignore the yellow waymarks from here on and go through the gate down into Parsonage Farm. The path goes through the farm buildings, keeping to the right hand side of the farmhouse and then carries on down the entrance road. This is a fine opportunity of seeing a typical Exmoor hill farm at close quarters to appreciate the difficulties of farming on the steep hills at this altitude. Follow the road as it turns left over a stream and then climbs again to a footpath sign at the end of the metalled road.

If only the shorter walk is being tackled, turn left here towards Tarr Steps but otherwise turn right and follow the road uphill to Tarr Post on the Withypool road, passing what was Hawkridge Common on the left. At Tarr Post turn left, then after 50 yards turn right down the entrance to Shircombe Farm.

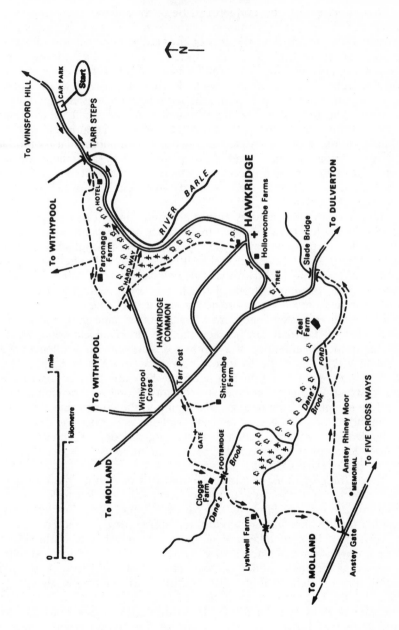

35

Straight ahead on the horizon can be seen Molland Common on the right and West Anstey Common to the left. This walk is heading for Anstey Gate, which is at the top of the hedge between the two commons, and route finding on this stretch is assisted by red waymarks. Follow the farm entrance road until it bears left and then climb the stile on the right. Turn ¾ left and walk down across the field to a green painted gate. Go through this into the large field on Wester Shircombe.

Turn right and follow the field boundary to the small valley beside Cloggs Farm. Follow the path down the valley to its junction with the Dane's Brook, which is crossed at this point by a substantial footbridge. Bridges at this site have had a chequered history and there are still traces upstream of the predecessors which were washed away. The present one was repaired as recently as 1978 with the help of helicopters of the Army Air Corps.

After crossing the bridge, turn right and climb diagonally up the gulley on the left between birch trees. When a low bank is met, follow this up left to the gateway in the top hedge. Go through this gate and turn left to pass on the left of Lyshwell Farm. Turn right after passing the generator buildings and then the path follows the farm entrance road to Anstey Gate, passing in front of the farmhouse, crossing a stream and then climbing onto open moorland through a steel gate.

On arrival at Anstey Gate, turn left across the cattle grid, and in front to the left of the road can be seen the Froude Hancock stone, erected by his friends in memory of a renowned stag hunting gentleman who died in 1933. The route to follow now is across Anstey Rhiney Moor towards Zeal Farm. Start off half left from the cattle grid on a well used track, which gradually becomes less distinct. However, the buildings of Zeal lie straight in front to assist in keeping to the correct line across this open moorland. This is easy downhill walking and, once the road is left behind, there is a good chance of sighting red deer. Over to the left below Shircombe Farm can be seen Shircombe Brake and the wild valley of the Dane's Brook.

About three-quarters of the way across this moorland, the path deviates slightly up to the right and then forks. Take the left fork here, still heading towards the farm. As the path nears the river, turn left onto a muddy track which leads down through dense gorse to Zeal Ford.

Turn right here to take any of the tracks which follow the Dane's Brook downstream to Slade Bridge. Turn left over the bridge and follow the road as it climbs steeply past the entrance to Zeal Farm. On the next bend, turn off right to follow the footpath sign pointing to Hawkridge, head for the large tree in the middle of the field and then turn ½ left to the gate in the corner of the field. Go through the gate onto the road and walk into Hawkridge. This is one of the highest communities on

Exmoor and was the last to be relieved after the freak blizzard of February 1978 when it was cut off from the outside world for 10 days.

At the village centre turn left on the road to Withypool and then turn right through the first gateway after the post office. Turn half left inside the gate and follow the direction indicated by the signpost for Tarr Steps to cross two fields before climbing a stile in the field corner. Keep to the left of the hedge and follow this boundary to the Parsonage Farm entrance road, where the less ambitious walkers left the longer walk. This section of the walk follows part of the route of the Long Distance Footpath between Exmoor and Dartmoor, 'The Two Moors Way'.

Turn right down the 'Hardway' signposted to Tarr Steps and descend steeply between oak tree on the left and conifers on the right to meet the road from Hawkridge at Penny Bridge. Turn left onto this little used road and follow it alongside the Barle back to Tarr Steps, passing some Chilean beech trees which have been planted to replace an avenue of firs. On reaching the clapper bridge, there remains just one more decision to be made. Which one of the party will volunteer to fetch the car from the car park?

Molland Common
3 miles (5 km)

OS sheet 181
Start: Anstey Gate (also known as Two Moors Gate), OS map ref. 835298

This is a relatively short walk, entirely on the open moorland of Molland Common. The distance is a nominal three miles, but it is possible to increase or decrease this as required because, except in winter, most of this area is 'walkable' at will. Molland Common is on the ridge which forms the southern boundary of Exmoor National Park and is a natural gallery to view the apparently limitless acres of rolling mid-Devon backed by the heights of Dartmoor on the horizon.

It is pointless to pick out individual points of interest on this walk because the enchantment is the depth of the view and the abundance of natural wildlife. This includes pure bred Exmoor ponies whose foals arrive in April and May, red deer, foxes, rabbits and birds of prey including rare sights of merlins and hen harriers.

An added attraction to this walk is the suggested route to approach the starting point by car. This route covers several of the lesser known roads and gives near and distant views which are some of the best to be obtained on Exmoor. Take the car to Simonsbath and then drive out on the road to South Molton. Turn left at Kinsford Gate and follow the county boundary along the ridge road to Sandyway Cross. (The highest public house in Exmoor – the Sportsmans Arms – is a few yards down the road to the left.) Turn right and immediately left. After ½ mile turn left again at Mudgate Cross and then, at White Post, turn right towards Molland. Turn left at Ridgeway Cross, and Anstey Gate is the next cattle grid. There is a car park on the right immediately after the grid. Alternatively, the start point can be quickly reached from Dulverton by taking the Hawkridge road to Five Cross Ways and then taking the Molland road. The car park is on the left three miles after Five Cross Ways just after passing the Hancock memorial stone on the right.

Starting off opposite the entrance road to Lyshwell Farm, take the track which is indicated by the footpath sign to Molland. This is not the wide one parallel to the road but the narrower one slightly to the left. The path steadily veers away left to the centre of the common and gently descends to cross the top of Anstey Combe. About 300 yards further on, the path crosses another path, edged by stunted bushes to the right.

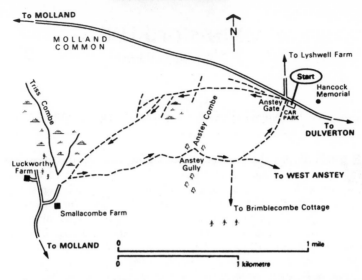

Carry straight on for nearly 200 yards, ignoring the first fork off to the left but veering left at the next fork. Keep on in the same general direction across another track and the path starts to descend gradually towards a row of fir trees on the opposite side of Triss Combe. Do not descend into the combe on the right but take any of the numerous tracks heading towards Smallacombe Farm to the left of the aforementioned row of fir trees.

As soon as the farm itself comes into sight, walk towards it. As the path descends more steeply through gorse it runs into a sunken track. Continue down this, still towards the farm, with a combe immediately down below on the right. Just after passing a small quarry on the left, there is a footpath sign on the right. Turn left here towards West Anstey and climb towards the boundary hedge, swinging left to keep the hedge and bank on the right.

It is a steady climb now up to a grassy corner of the common. Still keeping in touch with the boundary of the common the path descends into a minor combe, climbs out of it and then descends again to the deeper, birch lined Anstey Gully. The force of the water draining off Molland Common can be appreciated here by the deep crevices cut in the bottom.

Still proceeding in an easterly direction, climb out of the gully and, when the entrance to Brimblecombe cottage is reached, the path becomes a wide vehicle track. Follow this for 150 yards and then fork up left towards a tall hedge which leads back to the car park at Anstey Gate.

Winsford Hill
5½ miles (9 km)

OS sheet 181
Start: Winsford village car park, OS map ref. 906349

Winsford has the reputation of being one of the most beautiful villages in England and the residents try very hard to justify this reputation. It is also known as the 'village of bridges' with nine bridges of various sizes crossing the river Exe and the Winn Brook. In the centre there is plenty of evidence that the art of thatching is still not lost in Somerset. Another claim to fame is as the birth-place of Ernest Bevin, the wartime Minister of Labour who lent his name to the 'Bevin Boys' who were conscripted to work in the mines. Later Bevin became an eminent Foreign Secretary.

The village is easy to find on the wide road leaving the A396 at Coppleham Cross, just north of Bridgetown. This spacious road which runs from the A396 through Winsford, Exford and Simonsbath to the county border at Brendon Two Gates was the result of a 'job creation' scheme to relieve unemployment between 1926 and 1933. There is ample parking space in the village car park opposite the garage.

To start the walk, go past Bridge Cottage towards the War Memorial and turn right over the bridge beside the ford with the Winsford Craft Centre on the left. Walk on up Ash Lane, passing Winsford Church with its lofty square tower nearly 100 feet high, and more modern houses on the right hand side. Just after the last of these, there is a footpath sign on the left pointing the way to Winsford Hill via the Punchbowl. Take this path which is confirmed with yellow waymarks. After passing in front of a new house, the path takes a fairly level course through several fields. Be sure to use the gates that are waymarked.

The stream down to the left is the Winn Brook from which Winsford derives its name. The wood climbing up behind it is Burrow Wood. Eventually the path joins the entrance road to Withycombe Farm (a very common name for farms on Exmoor).

To the left at this point, there is a fine view into the heart of the Punchbowl. The path will follow the rim of this natural phenomenon. Go round the right hand edge of the farm building, following the yellow marks. Cross the wooden bridge over the stream, climb up a short stretch of concrete road and then turn sharp right to go through the gate on the

40

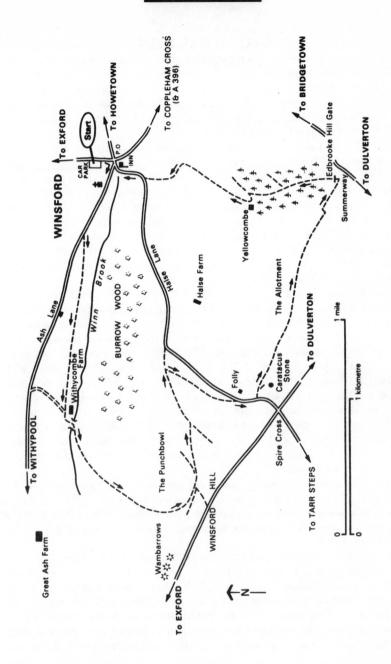

left. It is a steady climb now up to the highest point of the Punchbowl rim and it is well worth several pauses to look back at Winsford nestling in the Exe valley with the Brendon Hills in the background.

The next gate leads out onto the wide open spaces of Winsford Hill, held by the National Trust on a 499 year lease. Continue straight on uphill on a wide grassy track. To the right beyond Great Ash Farm can be seen the steep banks of the Exe Valley below Exford, and behind to the left, can be seen Dunkery Beacon.

The path steadily veers to the left, getting nearer to the edge of the Punchbowl. At the highest point there are paths joining from the right and here the yellow waymarking ceases. From here it is possible to make a short diversion by turning right up to the three Wambarrows which crown Winsford Hill at its highest point of 1399 ft. These are just three of the 300 or more barrows, or burial mounds, within Exmoor National Park, which are relics of the Bronze Age, lasting between 1600 BC and 500 BC. Only the more important men and women were buried in these graves and their numbers indicate the large population at that time when the climate was drier and warmer.

To continue the walk, return to the top edge of the Punchbowl and carry on round the edge for another 100 yards and then fork slightly right on a well used track. Slightly to the left on the horizon in front can be seen the WT mast on top of the Brendon Hills at Goosemoor.

After about ½ mile another path joins from the right and then as Howetown, a hamlet east of Winsford, comes into sight in the valley below, the path starts to descend slightly to the left before swinging round to the right towards the entrance to Halse Farm. Do not follow the path down to the road but turn right along a path which runs 200 yards above the Spire Cross to Winsford road (Halse Lane) and gradually draws nearer to it. Join the road opposite the house called Folly, follow it for 200 yards, and then turn sharp left as instructed by a footpath sign to Winsford.

After 50 yards go through a gate and then turn half right to cross The Allotment. If it is wished to take the opportunity of visiting the Caratacus Stone, it lies about 300 yards up the path to the right before passing through the gate. It will be found semi-concealed in the gorse to the right hand side.

This stone is of great historical interest because it is the only inscribed one in Somerset. It is believed to have been a guide or sighting stone before it was inscribed CARACTI NEPOC (Kinsman of Caratacus) in the 5th or 6th century to commemorate a notable person. It suffered its first vandalism in 1890 when the corner with the letter N on it was broken off with a pick. This fragment was found in 1906 when the present shelter was erected and fixed back on the next year. The whole stone was again vandalized in 1936 when it was dug out of the ground (all 7 cwt of it!), probably to satisfy local curiosity concerning the possibility of buried treasure beneath. In 1937 it was re-erected and has been successfully protected since then.

The path across the heather covered Allotment is level and nearly straight for a mile. This is a regular haunt for lapwing, curlew, skylarks and of course the ever present meadow pipits. As the conifers of Yellowcombe come into sight in front, the path gradually descends to pass through a small gate into Summerway.

Carry on in the same direction towards a disused pit on the left hand side of the field. Above this pit is a signpost which indicates that the path to Winsford is left through Edbrook Hill Gate along a wide forestry track. Now the path descends rapidly through the plantation. Very often rabbits can be seen scurrying around here and occasionally the cry of a cock pheasant can surprise when all else is quiet.

With Yellowcombe Cottage down below to the left, the track forks. Take the left track and then turn sharp left to follow waymarks leading down to a bridge. Cross the bridge and turn right. There is a steady pull up a sunken lane with overgrown hedges on both sides and occasionally, deep mud underfoot.

This path carries on climbing and then swings left to give a bird's eye view of all Winsford down below and Howetown away to the right. It is a steep downhill path now, on bare rock in places, to join the road into Winsford from Winsford Hill. Turn right onto this road passing the Karslake Hotel and the Royal Oak Inn en route for the car park.

The Exe Valley
8½ miles (13.5 km)

OS sheet 181
Start: Exford car park, OS map ref. 854384

Exford is near the geographical centre of Exmoor, and if Exmoor is 'the land of the horse', Exford can be considered the capital of that land. There are two hotels, both with extensive blocks of stables and plenty of other stabling in the village which is also the home of the Devon and Somerset Stag Hounds. In recent years, the final of the British Horse Society's 'Golden Horseshoe' endurance test for horses and riders has been based here in mid-May. Logically, the exercise of all these horses is only possible where there are plenty of bridleways and as these also serve as footpaths, walkers do benefit from all this equine activity! This may not be quite so obvious when the bridleways are deep in mud but in general there is a happy sharing of rights of way.

Exford is easily found on the B3224/B3223 between Wheddon Cross and Simonsbath, and the car park entrance is opposite the Crown Hotel in the village centre.

Starting from the car park, walk past the National Park Depot and through a kissing gate by a screen of rhododendrons. Keep to the river bank through the next two fields, noting the efforts which this farmer has made to replenish the hardwood trees. Turn right to cross the Exe river and follow red waymarks through the buildings of Court Farm, turning left, right and then left again to go through a gate into a lane on the side of a field. Follow this sunken lane upwards, go through one gate into a corridor then turn left after the next gate to continue on an enclosed track with a wire fence on the right and hedge on the left.

Go through a hunting gate, across a stream and then climb up a steep stony track with open hillside on the right and a small wood on the left. As the climb eases, the track enters an open field. Looking to the left, the outskirts of Exford can be seen with the church in the background. To the right of the church is Stone with the Rowbarrows on the horizon behind and Dunkery Beacon to the right. Half left, in the corner of a field below, can be seen the remaining earthworks of Road Castle, an Iron Age fort overlooking the river.

Keep straight on to a gate on the other side of the field, go through the gate and then turn right, climbing up again on Road Hill. Walk by

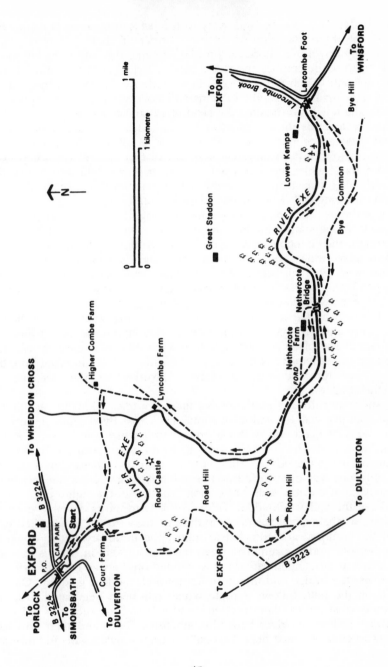

the hedge on the right, and away to the left can be seen Winsford Hill with the three Wambarrows on top. Further on there is a wild combe tumbling down from Room Hill to the Exe, and the path turns left round the head of the combe, opposite a solitary large beech tree in the hedge on the right. Then the path goes in a southerly direction with gorse on the right up to a signpost to Winsford. Follow the sign, sweeping left around a fence surrounding the head of a marshy combe.

Make towards the left hand end of a hedge which appears in front and then descend parallel with this hedge towards Nethercote Farm down below in the valley. The last part of this descent is a steep, well worn track which goes down to the river. Turn right and follow the riverbank downstream, going through a gate on the right by the ford and following yellow waymarks to Nethercote bridge.

For the next two miles of riverside walking, there is a good chance of seeing dippers and herons and possibly mink and kingfishers. Go through the hunting gate and out onto the farm access road at Nethercote bridge and continue in the same direction on the road. As recently as 1970 this stretch of the river Exe was considered as a possible reservoir site for the South West Water Authority but was reprieved when Wimbleball was selected.

The next bridge at Larcombe Foot is the turning point of the walk and is a very attractive site for a picnic with very little noise except the rush of water. The place gets its name from Larcombe Brook which joins the Exe on the other side of the bridge. The various boxes hanging from the trees are for tradesmen to leave deliveries for the residents of Nethercote!

About 20 yards before the bridge there is a track climbing back above the road just walked. Follow this track up across Bye Common, heading for the right hand end of the boundary wall which can be seen on the skyline above. The last few yards up to the stone wall are hard work but, having achieved this, there are no more long hard climbs on this walk. Turn half right to follow the red waymarks across the reclaimed grassland at the top of Bye Common. The hill to the right on the other side of the valley is Staddon Hill and the farm, in its enviable position facing south, is Great Staddon. Go through the next red waymarked gate off the common and turn left to follow the boundary hedge down to Nethercote bridge again. The steep track on the hill in front is the one which was descended earlier but is avoided on the way back to Exford.

Cross the bridge and then turn left through the first gateway. On this section the path follows a route which has been negotiated to avoid inconveniencing the farm residents and it is still marked with red way-marks. Follow the river bank through three fields and then turn half right to cross the next field diagonally. Pass through a gate and turn left on rejoining the right of way. Fork right on this well used track where it divides for the ford.

After passing the two small huts high above the track on the right, which are not observation posts but merely pump houses for water supplies, there are no signs of human habitation along this beautiful open valley walk. Eventually the wild cleave is left behind and two grass fields are crossed before Lyncombe Farm. Just before the farm on the left hand side is a very well preserved pack horse bridge leading up to the field below Road Castle. Unfortunately there is no public right of way over this bridge.

Go straight through the farmyard and up along the farm entrance road, ignore the yellow waymarked route to the left, fork left and then climb gradually to Higher Combe Farm. Turn left just before this farm and head down to the bridge at the bottom of the field. Cross the bridge and stile and climb up out of the combe. Walk across the middle of the field and also the next one, then follow the hedge on the right to the next gateway. Go through the gate and follow the track down to Court Farm. Turn right just before the bridge and retrace the first part of the walk along the river bank.

Withypool Common and Barle Valley

3 miles (5 km)

OS sheet 181
Start: Withypool - Village Car Park, OS map ref. 844354

Withypool is a compact, attractive village which has been established at this important river crossing for a very long time. The present road bridge is the first one north of Dulverton capable of carrying heavy traffic across the river Barle. R. D. Blackmore, the author of *Lorna Doone* frequently stayed here, and there is an original letter of his, reserving accommodation at the local inn, hanging on the bar wall inside the Royal Oak.

Withypool is an ideal walking centre with a wide variety of walks fanning out in all directions. It is adjacent to the wide open spaces of Winsford Hill to the south east and Withypool Common to the southwest. The best known path is the 4 mile riverside walk to Tarr Steps, but on this occasion a shorter walk is suggested which covers part of the common and the Barle valley.

The village is clearly signposted from Exford, only 3 miles away. From Dulverton, take the B3223 over Winsford Hill, turning left 8 miles from Dulverton just after the cattle grid at the boundary of this hill. To find the starting point drive over the bridge opposite the post office and the car park is on the right hand side. Start the walk by turning right out of the car park and right again on the Sandyway road. About 600 yards up the road, immediately after the entrance to Waterhouse Farm, fork right onto the waymarked path signposted to Landacre. The route is waymarked red throughout.

Follow the line of the overhead cables on the right across Waterhouse Common to a large tree in the corner of the field in front. After the tree, continue to follow the cable. To the left is Withypool Hill with a round barrow at its summit and a well preserved stone circle on the south facing side. The path enters high gorse and then descends on a stone covered track to the bottom of Knighton Combe.

Turn left before the stream, follow it for about 150 yards and then cross by a small ash tree. Climb up out of the combe on the steep track, bearing right towards the top of a conifer plantation, then follow the hedge on the right. Cross the entrance road leading to Knighton and Brightworthy Farms and up in front can be seen Brightworthy Barrows,

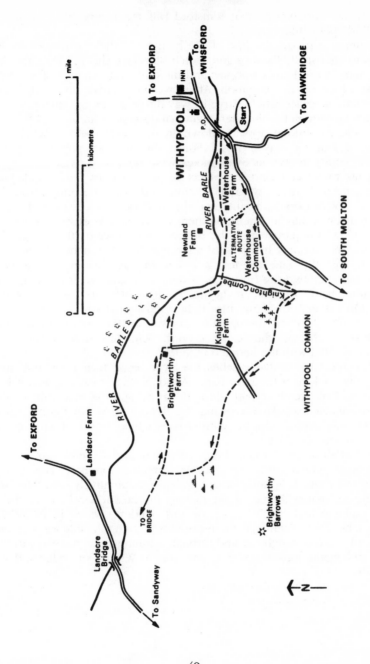

49

at 1404 feet, just higher than Winsford Hill and nearly 100 feet higher than Withypool Hill.

Continue to follow the line of the hedge. On the open moor to the left there are usually Exmoor and Scotch Blackface sheep. There are also large numbers of Exmoor ponies and there is a rare chance of seeing a fox or a hare on this common. After crossing a small stream the path rises a little more steeply to carve its way through a boggy stretch.

A few more minutes and then a gradual descent is started and the historic Landacre bridge appears down in the valley below. When the centre of Exmoor was a Royal Forest this was an important place because courts known as Swainmotes were held here twice a year for payments to be collected in respect of grazing dues, and regulations with regard to Forest Law to be administered. Now the bridge over the Barle is a very popular beauty spot because of its accessibility by car, and on a sunny Sunday afternoon there will be hordes of visitors here.

To follow this particular walk, do not make towards the bridge but keep to the boundary hedge until a footpath sign is reached. Turn right here through the gate and follow a sunken track leading all the way down into Brightworthy Farm. For wider views and easier walking, it is sometimes better to walk in the fields immediately to the right of the track. On reaching the farm, turn right opposite the stream gushing out of the wall. Go down through the gateway on the entrance road and then turn left through the next gate on the left. Head towards the river, walking parallel with the hedge on the left.

Just before this hedge reaches the river bank, turn right and then follow the track near the river bank. Although this is usually wet, it is a most attractive stretch of path along the Barle and the mud can usually be circumnavigated. After crossing the footbridge at Knighton Combe and climbing over a stile, the path crosses a field and then, after going through a gate, enters a lane.

There is a choice of routes here. Turn right and scramble up a stony watercourse which leads out onto Waterhouse Common. This is the shorter route but it is not pleasant walking. Alternatively turn left over the stile and across the next field, making for the left hand corner of the large building in front. Walk beside this building, which is an indoor riding school, and then pass through the next gate to a stile leading into a green lane. Go straight on and through a hunting gate to return to the river bank again, crossing over another stile to Withypool bridge and the car park.

Cow Castle
6½ miles (10.5 km)

OS sheets 180 and 181
Start: Birchcleave Wood, Simonsbath, OS map ref. 774393

Anybody who has travelled through Exmoor could be forgiven for expecting something different when they first arrived at Simonsbath. All roads seem to be signposted to the village from many miles away but the visitor can pass through in seconds without realizing he has seen all there is to be seen. It is the highest village on Exmoor in the largest parish with the smallest population.

Up to the early 19th century, there was only one building here and this is now the Simonsbath House Hotel. Originally it was the residence of the warden who was responsible for the administration of the Royal Forest of Exmoor. 'Forest' did not mean a densely wooded area but open country where game was preserved for hunting. In fact when a survey of Exmoor was made in 1814, the surveyor reported that there were only 37 trees in the moor, all growing around the warden's lodge. (He missed one which will be encountered on a later walk – the Hoar Oak.)

In 1818 it was decided to dispose of the Royal Forest and tenders were invited. The successful purchaser was a Mr. John Knight from Worcester who paid £50,000 for the 10,000 acres. This gentleman and his son Frederick endeavoured to create a farming and industrial community in the area, based on a new village built at Simonsbath. The full story of the 'reclamation' of Exmoor Forest is a fascinating saga and there is no dearth of informative books on the subject. Simonsbath lies 5 miles from Exford on the B3223 road to Lynton and 5 miles east of Challacombe on the B3358 road.

A car park together with toilets and a picnic area has been established down a turning opposite Birchcleave Wood.

Walk back to the road past what was the village school and the house that was the village post office stores. Turn right to pass Exmoor Forest Hotel, cross the road by The Pottery and enter Birchcleave Wood by the gate opposite. Inside the gate is a footpath sign. Follow the red way-marked path to Pickedstones, climbing through mature beeches planted by the Knights in 1840. At an altitude of 1300 feet, this is the highest known beech wood in the country and is approaching the end of its life. Replanting of beech and other species is now being carried out. But the storms of January 1990 decimated the mature trees in this wood.

51

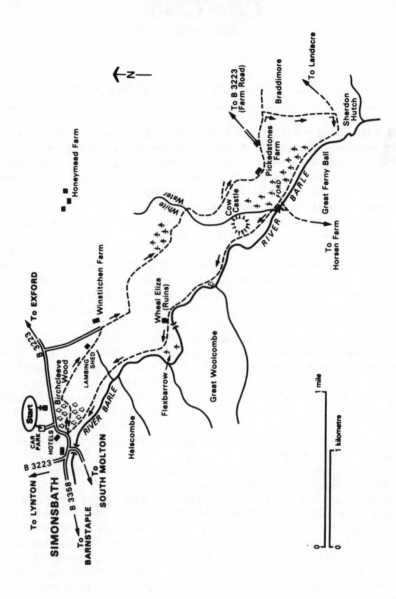

←N—

SIMONSBATH

To EXFORD

To LYNTON
B 3223

To BARNSTAPLE
B 3368

To SOUTH MOLTON

Start
CAR PARK
HOTELS

Birchcleeve Wood

LAMBING SHED

RIVER BARLE

Honeymead Farm

Winstitchen Farm

Wheal Eliza (Ruins)

Flexbarrow

Helscombe

Great Woolcombe

White Water

Cow Castle

FORD

RIVER BARLE

Pickedstones Farm

To B 3223 (Farm Road)

Braddimore

To Landacre

Sherdon Hutch

Great Ferny Ball

To Horsen Farm

1 mile

1 kilometre

0

0

52

At the top of the wood, turn left and walk about 250 yards to a gate on the right. Go through and follow the hedge to the next gate. Go through this and the one in front (not the one to the right). Now follow the bank on the right to the second gate. Turn left after going through this gate and follow a hedge down through two fields to a small lambing shed. Away to the right can be seen the heights of Halscombe and Great Woolcombe towering above the Barle valley.

Go through the hunting gate opposite the shed door and turn half left past tree stumps to join a track which has just passed Winstitchen Farm. Turn right onto the track and walk by a stone faced bank up to a gate on the left. Go through this and follow the hedge on the left through two fields to a plantation of conifers. Away to the left is the modern Honeymead Farm, built on the site of one of the original Knight farms. The patches of conifers dotted about have been planted principally to provide windbreaks and cover for the grazing livestock. Straight ahead can be seen the cairn of Brightworthy Barrows above the buildings of Pickedstones Farm.

Continue to follow the hedge on the left, veering left round the plantation, go through the gateway in front and turn right in the next field to follow a track down to the bridge over White Water. Turn right after passing through a gate on the other side and climb up the track to Pickedstones Farm. To the right is Cow Castle, an Iron Age defensive fort and to its left is the rocky outcrop known as the Calf.

Continue upwards with a wire fence on the right and, as the path levels out, go through two gates, crossing small streams between them. Follow the bank on the left and 200 yards further on turn left through a gate below the farmyard. Take the road out of the yard, passing the farmhouse and stables on the left. Follow the red waymarks to turn right off the road and follow the hedge on the right, veering slightly left at the end of the field to go through a gate out onto the open expanse of Braddimore. The three hills of similar shape in front from right to left are Brightworthy, Withypool and Winsford, all crowned with round barrows.

Turn right to leave the red waymarks and follow the moor boundary down to the second gate where there is a footpath sign for Landacre bridge which will have been seen to the left on the way down. Join the yellow waymarked path here and turn right through the gate towards Simonsbath. Down below is the Barle and Sherdon Water joining it to make a popular swimming pool at Sherdon Hutch. There is a pleasant steady descent to the gate into a large conifer plantation, with Cow Castle appearing again in front. Carry on through the wood and, when the track arrives at Horsen Ford, turn right towards the footbridge.

This is as good a place as any in which to take that overdue break for refreshment. More than half the walk has been completed and it is now a riverside walk nearly all the way back to Simonsbath. Access to Cow Castle is open and if, like so many others, you enjoy the peace and tranquility of the area, it is worth remembering that there is a shorter way to get here by taking the car along the public road to Horsen Farm, which lies off the Simonsbath to South Molton road. The path down to Cow Castle is signposted from the farm.

After the break, press on upstream, keeping on the east side of the river and crossing White Water by the footbridge. Keep to the left around the base of Cow Castle and go through a hunting gate adjacent to a river barrier. Continue along the bank to a row of beech trees. Go through the bank before the first tree and follow the path to the other end of the trees. Pass through the trees and turn right along the bank.

After the path has passed beneath a rocky outcrop, there is a wire fence on the left hand side, follow the fence, looking out for stonechats in one of their favourite haunts from May onwards.

Just before the next hedge, climb up through wild raspberries to go through a hunting gate. Down below are the remains of Wheal Eliza mine and, in front, the ruins of the miners' cottages. This is all there is to be seen of another venture of the Knight family when they mined for iron ore on the site of an ancient copper mine. Further information is available on the information board sited on the other side of the river.

After passing the cottages take the path to the right of the large natural mound in front, known as Flexbarrow. The river is soon in sight again and now the path hugs a steep hillside until it crosses the stream running down from the lambing shed which was passed on the outward walk. Be careful along here after rain because the path then becomes slippery.

Looking upstream, Simonsbath comes into sight round the edge of Birchcleave Wood. After passing through one hunting gate, there is a sunken track which can be avoided if too wet by walking on the bank above. This leads to another hunting gate into the wood and in a few minutes the starting point is reached.

Pinkworthy Pond and Chains Barrow
4 miles (6.5 km)

OS sheet 180
Start: Pinkworthy car park, OS map ref. 728402

Travelling between Simonsbath and Challacombe, the road follows one of the original tracks built by the Knight family in the early 19th century when they were reclaiming the old Royal Forest. This particular road was very important for the carriage of lime from north Devon ports, lime being essential to sweeten the sour moorland.

The high ground to the north is known as the Chains and claims an average rainfall of 80 inches per year. Most of the principal rivers in Exmoor originate from this peaty mass: the Barle and Exe running south to the English Channel, and Farley Water, Hoar Oak Water, and West Lyn running north into the Bristol Channel. Providing that normal care is used, it is possible to walk on this route without even getting wet feet but, as it is a very exposed walk, it is best to wait for a fine day with good visibility.

To find the starting point, drive west from Simonsbath on the B3358 towards Challacombe for 3 miles. Park the car in the first roadside car park on the right after the entrance to Driver Farm. Alternatively drive 2 miles east from Challacombe, and the car park required is the second on the left after the entrance to Pinkworthy Farm.

Start by walking on the wide verge towards Challacombe. The wild combe opposite the starting point leads up to a mysterious place known as Mole's Chamber. Here was once a very isolated inn, the Acland Arms, which was used by the miners who endeavoured to extract iron ore from this area. After passing through another car park the road swings right to the Pinkworthy Farm entrance.

To the left of the entrance gate there is a welcome sign to Pinkworthy Estate, through which this walk passes. This estate was purchased by Exmoor National Park in 1970 with the aid of a government grant after there had been a public outcry concerning proposals to plant conifer forests on the Chains in 1957. The whole of the estate is still traditionally farmed and Pinkworthy farm buildings have been developed into a renowned exploration centre, principally for the use of Somerset school children.

Walk up the drive to the farm with the infant Barle river on the left.

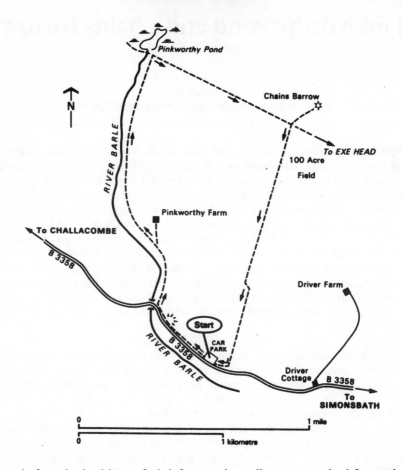

Just before the buildings, fork left onto the yellow waymarked footpath. Go through one gateway, veer right to go through another and head straight across the next field, gradually drawing closer to the river again. Go through a gate and then follow the well defined path which runs roughly parallel with the river to its origin in the face of the retaining dam for Pinkworthy Pond.

This damming up of the source of the Barle was yet another of the Knight family projects. It is not definitely known why this was undertaken but there are various theories which have backing by different historians. The most widely held is that the reservoir of water created was to be used for topping up a canal system over the Chains to carry iron ore down to the sea by water and rail. Others believe that it was

56

the basis of an irrigation system and yet another probability was the need for water to drive the pump machinery for the mines.

From the signpost at the eastern end of the dam turn right to follow the boundary bank, keeping to the south side of the bank for the best walking conditions. The path is traversing the Chains now and it was from here that the disastrous Lynmouth flood in 1952 originated. The moor was already saturated from a wet August and then a phenomenal thunderstorm sluiced off the waterlogged peat to cause unprecedented flooding both to the north and south.

There is a steady climb now up to Chains Barrow at 1598 feet. To visit the barrow, turn left at the four-way signpost and, walking towards the highest point, the triangulation point will soon be spotted. It is surrounded by single strand barbed wire to prevent further damage by cattle and ponies which range freely in this area. This is one of the best moorland viewpoints on Exmoor. Looking east over Long Chains Combe and Brendon Common, Dunkery Beacon is the hill on the skyline. To the south, Five Barrows can clearly be seen breaking the skyline and to the west there are long distance views into north and mid-Devon. With good visibility it is possible to spot the height of Brown Willy on Bodmin Moor in Cornwall.

Retrace the path back to the signpost and go through the gate in the wall. Walk across the field in the general direction of the sign pointing to the B3358 road – there should be marker posts to help keep straight. Unfortunately these posts are also used as rubbing posts by cattle and sheep with the inevitable result that there is rarely a complete set. This is a gradual descent through a very large (100 acre) field but as long as the markers are followed, there are easy walking conditions. Go through the yellow waymarked gate on the far side, turn left and follow the hedge boundary on the left through two fields back down to the road and car park.

Bossington Hill and Hurlstone
3 miles (5 km)

OS sheet 181
Start: Bossington Hill car park, OS map ref. 911477

Minehead may not be strictly part of Exmoor but its claim to be a 'gateway' to Exmoor National Park can certainly be justified. On its doorstep it also has North Hill, which is not only a beautiful area to traverse by car and explore on foot but provides the most perfect viewpoint for the northeast of Exmoor, especially the large areas of land given to the National Trust by Sir Richard Acland in 1944. Nearly all of North Hill itself is owned by the National Trust, West Somerset District Council and Exmoor National Park. Except on the cultivated land, there is free access for everybody and there are a multitude of paths including three levels of coast paths from Minehead to Burgundy Combe.

This walk starts from the car park at the extreme western end of the scenic road which runs the length of North Hill. To find this road from the centre of Minehead, travel down the parade towards the sea and turn left opposite W. H. Smiths. Take the first turning on the left, pass a car park entrance and the road is signposted to North Hill thereon, passing below the magnificent church and through Higher Town. It is well worth dawdling along this road – everyone else will be! To the right is the Bristol Channel stretching back to Weston-super-Mare and beyond, with the squat islands of Flat Holme and Steep Holme in the middle distance. On the other side of the channel is Wales, with views all the way into the Brecon Beacons on clear days. Straight behind are the Quantock Hills and to the left is Exmoor.

Running off the end of the tarmacadam road onto the loose stone of the car park, turn right into the portion which faces north. The start of the walk is at the east end of this car park where there is a signpost pointing to Hurlstone. Follow this path northwards. To the left, the small cairn marks the top of Bossington Hill, and the large cairn to the right is Selworthy Beacon, an ancient signalling site. Down below to the left is Bossington Beach with its wide variety of bird life and at the far end of the beach nestles Porlock Weir with Ashley Combe and then Culbone Woods behind. After this the wooded hogsback cliffs stretch away westward to Foreland Point.

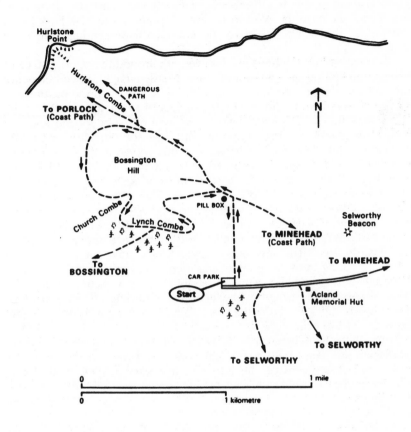

Keep to the wide track which bends slightly left by a wartime relic in the form of a concrete pillbox. Now, down to the left can be seen the sprawl of Porlock in the centre of the fertile Vale and at the foot of tree-lined Hawkcombe. Ley Hill is the nicely rounded hill just to the left of this combe. At a T-junction turn left, and now the Somerset and North Devon Coast Path has been joined. This is one of the Countryside Commission's long distance footpaths, and is itself part of the South West Peninsular Way which stretches from Minehead to Studland Bay in Dorset. An acorn sign is the recognition symbol for this long distance path.

From here, follow the Coast Path downwards to the top of Hurlstone Combe, passing the junction with an alternative route to Minehead. With good visibility, there is a fine view of the Welsh coast stretching from Port Eynon Point in the West to Lavernock point in the East. Fork left at the top of the combe to leave the coast path descending down the combe itself.

This next stretch is a most impressive path around the seaward face of Bossington Hill on the 350 foot contour. Nearly straight down below are the paths leading to the lighthouse and the beach. Then the picturesque village of Bossington followed by the hamlet of Lynch appear. When the wind is in the north or west, this is a favourite spot for the sport of hang-gliding and, walking along this path, it is not difficult to appreciate the view enjoyed by the participants in this sport. As the path sweeps inland the next village below in front is Allerford with its well known pack horse bridge, and on the horizon in front is Dunkery Beacon with Robin How and Joaney How to the left. The path continues around Church Combe, towards Porlock again, and then into the evergreen holm oak trees of Lynch Combe. Turn left towards Selworthy Beacon at the footpath sign in the combe and commence the steady climb homewards. Here it is very encouraging to see how many varieties of relatively young trees are establishing themselves in this sheltered spot. Although it is possible to struggle straight up, it is better to take the more gentle rising zigzag route which entails turning off left and heading towards the top of Bossington Hill and then right as soon as the cairn appears in front.

Turn right again when a wide track is reached and rejoin the outward path at a coast path acorn sign, forking off right again to pass the pillbox that was noted on the way out. It is easy to pick another way back over the last half mile, because the car park is visible for at least this distance.

Worthy Combe and Wood

4½ or 3 miles (7 or 5 km)

OS sheet 181
Start: Porlock Weir car park, OS map ref. 865479

Many years ago Porlock was a port, but the sea receded and a new port was established at Porlock Weir. Because of the indifferent road conditions on Exmoor, much use was made of the ports between Ilfracombe and Minehead by coastal traffic. The small boats delivered limestone, coal, woollen yarn, etc., and collected bark for tanning, timber and bricks. Today there is no commercial traffic but the harbour at Porlock Weir is now used by pleasure craft and as a base for sailing expeditions.

To get to the starting point take the B3255 road from Porlock and park on the car park opposite the Ship Inn, overlooking Porlock Bay. Here there are usually signs of the activity necessary to protect the harbour and preserve the protective shingle bank of Porlock Beach.

To start the walk, cross the road opposite the car park entrance and turn right behind the Anchor Hotel to follow the signs pointing to Culbone. Red waymarks confirm the route of the path as it passes through fields before joining the Worthy Toll Road. There are easy stiles to be negotiated on this stretch and provision is made for dogs beside the stiles. Turn right to follow the road for about 80 yards, then turn left opposite Worthy Manor on to a signposted bridleway which is now confirmed by blue waymarking. It will be noticed that this is the start of the alternative route to Culbone made necessary by landslips across the traditional route through Culbone woods.

The wide bridleway climbs steadily through coppiced woodland where the trees are predominately oak, ash, chestnut and sycamore. After passing Lovelace Cottage it runs parallel with the stream of Worthy Combe and the Worthy toll road down below to the right. In the storms of early 1990 the hurricane-force winds completely blocked this route and the scars of the work necessary to clear it by heavy machinery will be seen for a very long time. The disused shed to the right still contains tanks which held preservatives for the timber extracted in this area. About 120 yards after passing a farmhouse, on the other side of the road, there is a 'T' junction – time for a breather here! Turn left to follow yellow waymarks along a wide track. This track is legally a 'road', so it is possible to encounter vehicles along this stretch.

It is a steady ascent now to the highest point of the walk, approximately

PORLOCK WEIR

WORTHY

To PORLOCK
Toll Road
West Porlock
Porlockford
B 3225
To MINEHEAD (Coast Path)
Porlock Beach
Start
DOCK CAR PARK
DOCK
Worthy Manor
Worthy Wood
Short Walk
Longer Walk
Eastcott Bridge
Yearnor Mill Bridge
Worthy Combe Toll Road
To Pitt Farm

YEARNOR WOOD

CULBONE
Culbone Combe
Ash Farm
Yearnor Farm
Parsonage Farm
To Culbone Stables Inn (A 39)

To County Gate (Coast Path)
Silcombe Farm

1 mile
1 kilometre
N

750 feet above sea level. The woodland on the left is more open and there are good chances of spotting the native red deer or the smaller, shy roe deer. To the right, the rough grazing and bracken behind the wire fence is home for a multitude of rabbits. About ½ mile (10-15 minutes) after joining this track, there is a signpost indicating the route of a red waymarked path back to Porlock Weir. This is the route to follow for the shorter alternative walk.

This shorter walk follows a sunken path which passes through coppiced oak and a profusion of whortleberry plants. It becomes a wider track above a deep combe. Cross the combe to stay on this wide track and then turn sharp left down a narrow stony path, still indicated by the red waymarks, zig-zagging downwards fairly steeply to join the road above Porlock Weir. Turn right downhill on the road and then sharp left at the next junction to return to the car park.

To continue the longer walk, carry straight on towards Porlock. The track is joined by another path from the left and then a signposted junction is reached. The vehicle track continues straight on towards Porlock Weir but our route turns right to continue on the yellow waymarked route. It is a steady descent now with fields to the right at first and spectacular glimpses of Porlock Bay down below to the left. The next landmark is Eastcott Bridge where the path joins a wide track again. Turn right along this track although, yet again, it is possible to abbreviate the walk by turning left to follow the track towards Porlock Weir. Spectacular Porlockford Combe is crossed at Birchanger Bridge and at this point the Porlock to Pitcombe Head toll road is joined.

Turn sharp left to follow this road downhill. It is the gentle alternative to the steep climb of the A39 up Porlock Hill and for its scenic value is well worth the nominal toll which is levied by the private owners at the Toll House further up the road. As a privately owned road it is occasionally used for section trials during motor vehicle rallies but there is always very adequate warning if one of these events is taking place. Follow the road for about ten minutes and then, just as it bends sharply to the right with the vista of Porlock Bay and Hurlstone Point in front, turn left onto a red waymarked path.

The path descends fairly steeply through woodland, sweeping right and then carrying straight on across two forestry tracks (follow the red waymarks when in doubt!). Eventually a four way signpost is reached above West Porlock. Turn left here to follow the rather muddy path signposted to Porlock Weir. Cross the footbridge at Porlockford, turn right beside a large building to cross a minor road. Then, after a short stretch of path, the main road to Porlock Weir is reached, near its junction with the Worthy toll road. Depending upon the traffic and your personal choice, either of these roads can be used for the short distance back to the car park starting point.

To Dunkery Beacon from the East
6 miles (9.5 km)

OS sheet 181
Start: Brockwell, nr. Wootton Courtney, OS map ref. 928432

One of Exmoor's greatest assets is the widespread land ownership by the National Trust. There is unlimited public access to the open moorland and most of the woodland owned by them and this is seen to its very best advantage on the 12,000 acre Holnicote Estate. The largest part of this estate was given to the National Trust by Sir Richard Acland in 1944 and together with the other gifts of moorland made by Colonel Walter Wiggin and Mrs. Allan Hughes, covers an area from Selworthy Beacon in the north to Dunkery Gate in the south, and from Alderman's Barrow in the west to Brockwell in the east.

This suggested walk with the four following are all contained within the estate, but there are so many paths and bridleways, it would be possible to walk for a fortnight or more on different routes. Many of the paths are still known by the names given to them by the Acland family, particularly the tenth Baronet who lived from 1787 to 1871. This walk is all on open moorland and because of the views, particularly from the top of Dunkery Beacon, it would be as well to pick a fine day with good visibility.

To find the start point, drive into Wootton Courtney from the A396, Dunster to Tiverton road, leaving it at a point just north of Timberscombe. Go past the village shops and just after passing the Dunkery Hotel on the right, turn left down a dead end road signposted to Brockwell and Ford. Where the road to Ford swings off to the left, there is a National Trust sign and a three-way signpost. Park near here without obstructing farm entrances please.

Follow the arrow pointing towards Webber's Post and start off on a road up to a small bridge. After crossing the bridge, take the path signposted to Webber's Post again. There is a narrow uphill stony path at the start, but this soon comes out onto the open hillside. Now the track goes in a general westerly direction, veering left round some dense gorse to join a wider well-used track which passes below first Joaney How and then Robin How above to the left.

Away to the right is Porlock Vale with Selworthy Beacon above the unmistakable white Selworthy Church. As the path skirts around the top

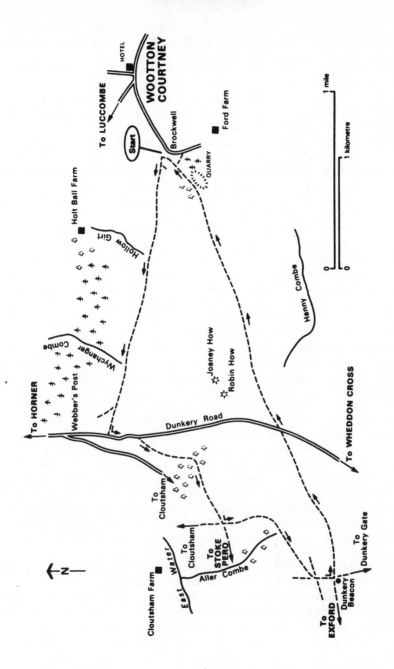

of a depression called Hollow Girt, the compact farm to the right is Holt Ball and further on to the right is the attractive village of Luccombe surrounding its 15th century church.

With conifer woods down to the right and Ley Hill appearing in front, it is a steady climb now to skirt the top of Wychanger Combe. Down to the right in front are the spacious car parking areas at Webber's Post which is the starting point for the short Walk 18. Carry straight on, and do not veer off to Webber's Post.

When the path strikes the Dunkery road, turn left and walk up the road for about 300 yards and then turn right along a path signposted 'Dicky's Path to Stoke Ridge'. Down to the right is the magnificent Horner valley, with Horner Water curling round Ley Hill and joining up with East Water below Webber's Post. Away up in front is the cairn of Dunkery Beacon, the next objective.

The path plunges down into a wooded combe and climbs out the other side. The track that can be seen down below in the woods is part of the well known Cloutsham Nature Trail. As the path comes out of the trees (still climbing!), the splendid farmhouse over to the right with its unusual verandahs is Cloutsham Farm. Fork left where the path splits and opposite the farmhouse, the path crosses another. Turn left here towards the left of Dunkery Beacon, starting off on a short grassy stretch which soon changes to a narrow stony path.

The path bears right around the head of Aller Combe and then heads for the cairn which can be seen from this point. On reaching the summit it will be seen that the cairn commemorates the handing over of Dunkery Beacon to the National Trust. This hill at the highest point in Exmoor has been used as a beacon for hundreds of years and the last royal occasion was in 1981, when the wedding of the Prince and Princess of Wales was celebrated with a chain of beacons throughout the British Isles. The all round views are too numerous to mention and it is best to check with the view point indicator adjacent to the cairn.

To set off on the return trip, head eastward along a wide track leading towards Brent Knoll – 27 miles away! This is the hill adjacent to the picnic area on the M5 between Bristol and Taunton. The amount of wear on these Dunkery paths is an insoluble problem for the National Trust because there is not enough soil on top of the bedrock to withstand the thousands of feet that pound the path every year.

On reaching the road, go straight across, and the path can be seen out in front running to the right of Robin and Joaney How. Away to the right are the Brendon Hills beyond Wheddon Cross. The large deep combe to the right is Hanny Combe, the principal source of water for the River Avill which passes through Timberscombe and Dunster.

On the last stretch of path across the moor, detailed directions are hardly necessary because Wootton Courtney can be seen directly in front. However do be careful here because water has badly eroded the path in places and it is best to pick a way round these miniature ravines keeping to the right where alternatives veer off to the left. At the bottom, the path passes tall gorse and birch trees with a disused quarry to the right, and then a plantation of larch surrounded by hardwoods. After this there is a red earth track and down below to the left is the car parking area, so turn off left just as an open space is reached.

Horner Hill
2¼ miles (3.5 km)

OS sheet 181
Start: Webber's Post car park, OS map ref. 903438

This is the second of the walks on the National Trust Holnicote Estate and is a lot less strenuous than Walk 17. It is just long enough to put an edge on the appetite for a picnic at Webber's Post itself which must be one of the most beautiful areas set aside for car parking in the whole of Exmoor National Park.

To find the start point from the A39, turn off ¾ mile east of Porlock onto the road signposted to Horner. Go through Horner Green and at the next crossroads (Chapel Cross) turn right towards Cloutsham and Dunkery Beacon. Fork right to Cloutsham and 200 yards further on pull on to the car park on the right. Alternatively, travelling from Wheddon Cross on the Exford road, fork right to Dunkery about ½ mile from Wheddon Cross, go over the cattle grid at Dunkery Gate, travel over the top of the hill and slowly descend to the junction with the Cloutsham road. Turn sharp left on to this and then after 200 yards pull on to the car park on the right. If Walk 17 is not to be attempted, it is well worth stopping on the way down from Dunkery to take in the magnificent view down to the right of Bridgwater Bay and beyond.

On the car park there is a National Trust collecting box and sign under a pine tree. From here, with back to the road, walk towards the edge of the parking area and look down into the Horner valley. The dense oak coppice woods are especially preserved as a unique site of special scientific interest because they have not been cut back for over 100 years. Normal coppice practice is for the trees to be cut back, allowing the shoots which spring from the stump to grow for a period of time (7 to 30 years depending upon site, species and intended use). This can be repeated indefinitely and was common local woodland management from the Middle Ages until the mid-19th century. It is still practised occasionally to provide posts for cleaving into long lasting fence posts.

This is a splendid vantage point, and during the deer hunting seasons the valleys below are a natural amphitheatre for the many spectators who congregated here. The deer hunting seasons are as follows: in the autumn those stags which are at least five years old (as evidenced by their antlers) are hunted; in October the mating season – 'the rut' –

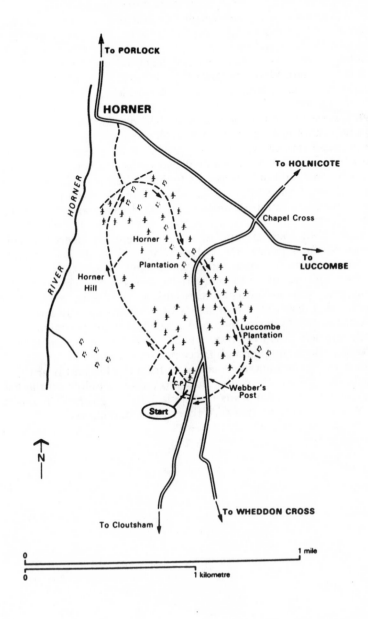

To PORLOCK

HORNER

To HOLNICOTE

RIVER HORNER

Chapel Cross

Horner

Plantation

To
LUCCOMBE

Horner
Hill

Luccombe
Plantation

C.P.

Webber's
Post

Start

N

To Cloutsham

To WHEDDON CROSS

0   1 mile

0   1 kilometre

begins and from then until the end of February hinds are hunted; in the spring it is the turn of the younger stags to be hunted.

Turn right down an uneven path to skirt below a small plantation of fragrant Scots pine and keep on in a general northerly direction, down through tall gorse and then steadily climbing to join the main path from Webber's Post to Horner. There is no signpost here but turn left towards Horner and now down below to the left can be seen the two distinct valleys of Horner Water and East Water which join forces immediately below. Another plantation of pines is passed on the right and then the path enters an open stretch of land which is deliberately cut back to provide a fire-break in this high fire risk area.

Still heading north and passing 'Susan's Seat', there are now views to the right of Porlock Vale and North Hill. The heather topped hill to the left is Ley Hill, and in front is Crawter Hill. The track narrows as it enters the next lot of pines but there is still a fire-break to the left. Now immediately in front is the distinct profile of Bossington Hill with Porlock down below.

As the path goes through larger pines, there is a steeper descent to a signpost which points left to East Water. Turn right here and keep straight on towards Chapel Steep at the next signpost. 30 yards further on turn right again to follow 'His Honour's Path'. This is one of the many paths named and enjoyed by the Acland family before the estate was handed over to the National Trust. It climbs steadily through mixed woodland, mostly Scots pine and silver birch. Keep straight on to the road, turn left down the road for 25 yards and then turn right onto a vehicle track passing through Luccombe Plantation.

Bear right when another track joins from the left and bear right again where there is a path leading down to a combe below on the left. In a few minutes the path leads to a pole barrier, go through this and in front is the eastern section of Webber's Post parking area.

Horner Wood
4 miles (6.5 km)

OS sheet 181
Start: Horner car park, OS map ref. 898455

The next walk on the Holnicote Estate starts from the more formal car park in the hamlet of Horner. This attractively laid out car park complete with toilets is the result of co-operation between the National Trust as owners of the land and the National Park Authority who have provided the facilities to preserve Horner Green itself. This very small community is a miniature rest and recreation centre with riding stables, farm accommodation and a cafe. Walks radiate in all directions and tickets for fishing in Horner Water are obtainable from one of the cottages facing the green.

To find Horner from the Wheddon Cross direction, follow the directions given for Webber's Post in the previous walk and carry straight on when the Cloutsham road joins from the left. Go downhill across the cattle grid and turn left at the crossroads. The car park entrance is at the other end of Horner. From the A39, turn off on the road signposted to Horner ³/₄ mile east of Porlock and the car park is on the left just after passing the caravan park at Burrowhayes.

To start the walk, leave the car park by the vehicle entrance, turn left to walk along the road for 40 yards, then turn right to cross the pack horse bridge over Horner Water. This is a very well preserved specimen of this type of bridge, which is built well clear of the water in order that debris brought down when the river is in full spate does not build up against the buttresses.

Turn right after the bridge and then after only 25 yards turn sharp left to climb up a path which runs above the water. Straightaway the path enters mature woodland with some very large oak and ash trees. The gradient is not too demanding and very soon the large scout camp site can be seen in the meadow below to the left.

Still climbing, the path veers away from the stream and then swings left around the head of a more open combe with a good view of the pine trees near Webber's Post on the other side of the valley. All along this path is evidence of the extensive work carried out by the National Trust with the help of a 'job creation' team to maintain it in a good state for both walker and rider. After a narrow stretch of path which is criss-

71

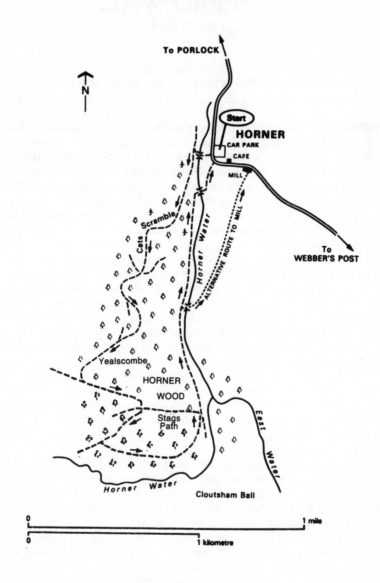

To PORLOCK

N

Start
HORNER
CAR PARK
CAFE
MILL

To
WEBBER'S POST

Scramble
Cats
Horner Water
ALTERNATIVE ROUTE TO MILL

Yealscombe
HORNER
WOOD
Stags
Path

East Water

Horner Water
Cloutsham Ball

0   1 mile
0   1 kilometre

72

crossed by the roots of adjacent trees, another wider path is crossed. Keep straight on and the next landmark is a very welcome bench on the right.

Again the path sweeps left around the head of a wooded combe and after this the trees are nearly all coppiced oak. Keep on the main path and do not fork off on other tracks to the right. At the next signpost keep straight on, and it will be noted that the 'Cats Scramble' has been successfully negotiated from Horner. It is hard to believe that it was only ³/₄ mile! There is another bench on the right, strategically placed to take advantage of magnificent views of Webber's Post to the left and Joaney How in front.

As another path crosses from right to left, veer left onto this path to sweep round the head of wooded Yealscombe. Following the edge of this combe, the next views to the left are of Bossington Hill, Allerford and just a glimpse of Selworthy with the beacon behind.

Now the path which is known as 'Granny's Ride' descends steadily and Dunkery Beacon can be glimpsed through the trees to the left. Keep straight on where Stags Path crosses but if it is wished to shorten the walk, turn left down Stags Path which descends steeply to the track near the junction of Horner and East Waters.

After a short steep stretch Granny's Ride joins a wide vehicle track; turn sharp left on to this track and follow it downhill. It was originally excavated to enable foresters to carry out the essential maintenance work to preserve the woodland. Although it scarred the landscape at first, nature is very rapidly softening its appearance and the well-being of the trees above are evidence of its benefit. The track provides easy downhill walking, passing through a wide vehicle turning area where it is joined by the path following Horner Water on the right and Stags Path from the left. Carry straight on now to follow the stream all the way back.

On the right where there are signs to Cloutsham, is the East Water which joins Horner Water at this point. From here on the track is very wide and well used because it is the level route used by the majority who do not wish to unduly exert themselves!

It is possible to cross the stream at the next bridge where there is a sign for Horner Mill and follow the mill leat back to Horner, but it is easier going to follow the main track. Next on the right, the scout camping area can be seen at close hand. Then the path goes through only the second gate on this walk, turns right over another stone bridge and Horner Green is just in front with the café a hundred yards away to the right, and Horner Mill a little further on.

East Water and Stoke Wood
4 miles (6.5 km)

OS sheet 181
Start: Cloutsham Ford, OS map ref. 897430

L ike the preceding walk, this one can be undertaken when the weather
is unsuitable for open moorland walking and is especially useful when
fog or low cloud is spoiling the visibility elsewhere. It is nearly all
amongst the trees of the Holnicote Estate and offers good chances of sighting red deer and a wide variety of woodland birds. The river bank west of
Cloutsham Ford has been a favourite picnic site for many years and is ideal
for those who do not wish to travel far from their cars because it is possible to park alongside the water in fields or near the road.

Cloutsham is reached from Webber's Post (see Walk 18 for directions to
Webber's Post). Follow the road from there signposted to Cloutsham and
park beside the road after crossing the ford. Alternatively Cloutsham can
be reached from Exford by travelling on the Porlock road passing the post
office, travelling uphill and then forking right immediately after crossing the
cattle grid to follow the signs via Stoke Pero Common and Cloutsham Farm.

On the west side of the ford there is a footpath sign to Horner. Follow
this path which sticks closely to East Water – crossing six footbridges on
the way! These have all been recently rebuilt by the National Trust to
enable not only riders but walkers to keep their feet dry. Near the first
bridge, old stone quarry workings presented a danger to passers-by and
this danger has been eliminated by a barrier of stones housed in wire
cages. These look somewhat incongruous in this setting, but they are
probably more efficient than a formal wall and eventually they will blend
with the background.

After crossing the sixth bridge, keep to the path nearest the stream and
then cross the next bridge over Horner Water. To the right from this
bridge can just be seen the junction of Horner and East Waters. Turn left
immediately after this bridge and follow the wide track up the side of
Horner Water for just 100 yards. Then take the first fork on the left and
continue to follow the stream on the same side but on a narrower path.
Up above on the right is a large clearing which was excavated for the use
of forestry vehicles. Just after passing a footbridge the path rejoins a wide
track again and a little further on there are wire enclosures on the right
protecting young trees from the depredations of the red deer which
abound in this area.

74

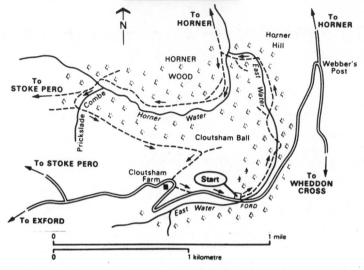

Look out for the next footbridge on the left and cross over it. Turn right towards Stoke Pero as indicated on the signpost and now the path climbs quite steeply away from the water. About 400 yards after the bridge take the first path sharply off to the left. This is less distinct than the Stoke Pero path but it is fairly wide and is not difficult to spot as it climbs up through the oaks beside steep-sided Prickslade Combe to the left. At the head of this combe, with an open field in front, turn left to cross the small stream, and the path carries on through woodland with a stone wall to the right.

The highest point of this walk has now been reached and there are glimpses through the trees on the left of the beautiful Horner valley. The steep valley side immediately to the left confirms that the climb up the side of Prickslade Combe was quite an achievement!

The path descends to skirt the top of the next combe and then climbs sharply again by the side of the wall to the right. As the path emerges into the open for the first time, stay close to the wall. Over to the left beyond Horner Woods is Porlock Vale with Bossington Hill and the sea beyond. Turn right through the next gate on the right and follow the wall on the left. Away to the left is Dunkery Beacon with the cairns at Robin How and Joaney How further to the left again.

After just one field go through a gate into a short lane which leads to the road skirting Cloutsham Farm. The unusual appearance of this farmhouse was created a hundred years ago when the eleventh Baronet built an extension onto the existing farmhouse in the 'Swiss' style. At the apex of this hairpin bend, turn off left down a rough track and follow this down to the road and picnic areas beside the water. On reaching the road carry straight on for the ford where the car is.

To Dunkery Beacon from the West
4 miles (6.5 km)

OS sheet 181
Start: Stoke Pero Common, OS map ref. 878427

This is the last of the five suggested walks contained within the National Trust Estate of Holnicote. It is similar to Walk 17, traversing open country to ascend Dunkery Beacon from the opposite direction. Again, it is recommended that this walk be undertaken on a day of good visibility. There is no danger of getting lost in mist but the long distance views are a feature not to be missed. This is probably the walk where sighting a wide variety of moorland bird life is most likely. Grouse, curlews and stonechats are frequently seen, ring ouzels are occasionally spotted and even the rare merlin is to be seen by a lucky few. Red deer are plentiful in the wooded combes and on the heather covered slopes. It is rare for the observant walker not be rewarded by a sight of these noble animals during a walk in this area.

From June onwards there is the added bonus of the fragrant heather flowering season which climaxes in August with the masses of ling or common heather forming a carpet of pale purple. Before this there is the cross-leaved variety with its globular pink drooping flowers and then the bell variety which favours drier ground and has crimson-purple, egg-shaped flowers.

The starting point is not a formal car park but it is not difficult to find. From Exford, take the Porlock road and fork right for Stoke Pero and Cloutsham after the cattle grid. After another ½ mile carry straight on towards Cloutsham and 1½ miles further on, just before a row of fir trees on the left, there is a pole barrier across a path on the right with a signpost which indicates that this is the start of Dicky's Path to Webber's Post. Park the car just off the road on the grass verges.

Follow Dicky's Path down into Bagley Combe, and up the other side. From here the cairn at the summit of Dunkery Beacon cannot be seen and the two cairns immediately in front are those on top of Robin How and Joaney How. Over to the left is Selworthy Beacon and half left the islands of Flat Holme and Steep Holme can be seen in Bridgwater Bay. Ignore the signposted path forking right to Dunkery Beacon and carry straight on. The path descends into and climbs out of another combe and then passes a row of beech trees on the left. Keep to the main track

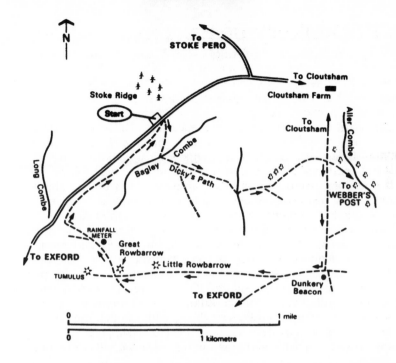

and pass to the right of two wire enclosures which are protecting barrows (Bronze Age Burial Grounds). After an easy stretch of level walking, the beeches end and it is possible to see Cloutsham Farm down below to the left, and the rocks of Hurlstone Point behind. Half left are the pines of Webber's Post with Selworthy church behind.

Just before descending the next combe another path crosses Dicky's Path. Turn right onto this path and commence the real climb to Dunkery Beacon. This is a fairly steep grassy path and perhaps the most pleasant way of tackling it is in short bursts with frequent about turns to appreciate the marvellous vista to the north. The deep combe to the left is Aller Combe and on the other side of this can just be seen the other route which was followed to Dunkery Beacon on Walk 17. Because of the shape of the hill, the cairn at the top does not appear until 100 yards from the summit, just after the steepest part of the ascent. At the summit, the view point indicator is the best help for identifying the numerous points of interest.

The walk now sets off on the homeward journey and the next target is westward to the Rowbarrows. The path is quite distinct and can be seen running along the ridge of the hill to two cairns marking the

77

position of these barrows which are one mile away. Walk past Little Rowbarrow and turn right to pass the left hand side of Great Rowbarrow on a grassy track leading towards a small wire enclosure. Quarter right is Porlock Hill and immediately in front is Lucott Moor draining down into Nutscale reservoir which provides Minehead's water supply. To the left are the wide open spaces of the heart of Exmoor, north of Simonsbath.

Pass just to the left of the small enclosure which surrounds a rainfall measuring gauge and follow the right hand path downwards to the Exford-Cloutsham road which it strikes by a National Trust collecting box at the head of Long Combe. Turn right here to follow the grassy path running parallel to the road, and very soon the car should be in sight again. This path does become very narrow through tall heather and if it is wet, perhaps it is better to walk down the road.

Over to the left is Stoke Pero with its very interesting church. At more than 1000 feet above sea level, this is the highest and most isolated church on Exmoor. It is also possible that this was the site of the first Christian church on Exmoor. Many restorations have taken place and one of these at the end of the 19th century is commemorated by a plaque recording the service of Zulu, a Porlock donkey who carried all the roof timbers up from Porlock. If the path through the heather is followed, it enters a gully which can be rather slippery. Do not plunge down here too quickly and look out for holes washed out by rain.

Hawkcombe

3½ miles (5.5 km)

OS sheet 181
Start: Pittcombe Head picnic area, OS map ref. 842463

One of the best-known features for motorists visiting or passing through Exmoor is the 'fearsome' Porlock Hill. Since 1900, when this was first climbed by a motor vehicle it has presented a challenge to hundreds of thousands of drivers. It holds no fear for the modern-day motorist but, to those who do not wish to risk being held up by a coach or juggernaut grinding up in bottom gear, there is the pleasure of using the toll road with its gentle gradients and beautiful scenery. If a caravan is being towed, the toll road gradients of 1 in 12 are much more reassuring than the stretch of 1 in 4 on the main road. The Porlock area generally is a maze of walks with open moorland, woodland owned by the National Park Authority and many miles of rights of way to choose from.

This walk starts from the picnic area at Pittcombe Head which is opposite the AA box at the junction of the A39 and the top of the toll road. As this car park is slightly concealed from the road, please ensure that the car is locked before leaving it. This is a cardinal rule in the more isolated Exmoor car parks because 'the ungodly' have been known to wait for the arrival of keen-looking walkers, knowing that they will have an undisturbed hour or two with an unattended car.

To start this walk, cross the A39 road to the AA box. Walk alongside the road towards Porlock for about 50 yards and then turn right to follow a wide track running parallel with a hedge on the right. Immediately to the left is the site of a 'knapping floor', where flints for hunting were worked by Stone Age man in the Neolithic period nearly 4000 years ago.

Do not fork up left to a triangulation point but keep straight on and turn left about 100 yards before an electricity supply line crosses the path. Just along here a level shelf running east-west is crossed. This is part of the remains of the preparations for a railway line to carry iron ore from Simonsbath in the centre of Exmoor to Porlock Weir. Two-thirds of the route was prepared but no rails were laid because the mines did not yield up to expectation.

Cross the Porlock-Exford road and follow the path indicated by the

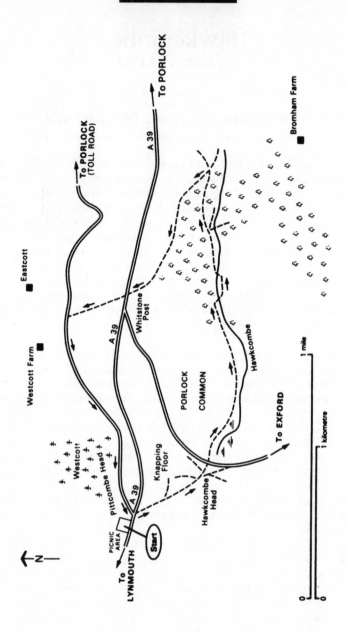

signpost for Porlock. This point is Hawkcombe Head and the patches of green rushes show where the springs rise to feed this combe. As the path descends along the side of the combe, Porlock Vale appears in front with Bridgwater Bay beyond. The trees mark the boundary of the land owned by the National Park Authority, and it will be noticed that the oaks' efforts at self-regeneration have been retarded by grazing animals, principally deer.

When the path meets the water again, do not cross it but take the path along the bank. Now the woodland is dense and in summertime the warblers' song is never ending. The main stream is joined by a small tributary from the left. Cross over the stream here to walk down the right hand side and avoid a scramble over stone scree. From here follow the stream downstream on the most convenient side until a four-way signpost is reached. The next path to follow is the red waymarked one signposted as Porlock via North Terrace. This starts off as a wide vehicle track which soon fords a small stream and then continues straight on, climbing more steeply with Bromham Farm visible through the trees on the right.

When the path emerges from the trees turn sharp left onto a narrow path signposted to Whitstone Post. Before starting along this path, there are good views back along the combe which has been followed and behind to Dunkery Beacon with the Rowbarrows to the right. The path now follows the edge of the woodland as it climbs steadily upward and out onto the open common. Keep straight on, heading for the Porlock road which can be seen crossing the horizon in front. Nearing the road, fork up right towards the junction of the A39 and the Exford road. Go straight across the A39 and follow the wide track heading towards the sea. Hop across the shallow ditch and bank, which is maintained to prevent cars encroaching from the car parking area.

After a steady descent through a mass of heather with a magnificent view of Porlock Beach, Hurlstone Point and Selworthy Beacon to the right, the path strikes the toll road from Porlock to Pittcombe Head. Turn left here and follow the road back to the car. Except during the peak holiday period this is not a busy road.

Weir Water and Pitt
4½ miles (7 km)

OS sheet 181
Start: Robber's Bridge car park, OS map ref. 823465

Many visitors associate Exmoor with Lorna Doone, the romantic novel written by R. D. Blackmore and set in the Exmoor of the late 17th century. From this novel, the exploits of the legendary Doones have been so publicized in the form of films and television series, that the visitors' curiosity leads them to the 'Doone Country' during their visit to Exmoor. At the beginning of the book, John Ridd's father is killed by the Doones as he returns to Plovers' Barrow farm from Porlock market. Perhaps the author had the beautiful setting of Robber's Bridge in mind for this dastardly deed.

Even if a walk is not contemplated, this peaceful stretch of valley is recommended for a visit at any time of the year. If complete peace is required, it is possible to roam freely over the eastern side of wild Mill Hill which is owned by the National Park Authority. The entrance to this piece of moorland is by the gate upstream from Robber's Bridge on the south side of the water.

To find Robber's Bridge, take the turning off the A39, 5½ miles from Lynmouth on the Somerset side of County Gate. This is signposted to Oare and Malmsmead. On reaching Oare church, turn left and travel along the narrow road for about 1½ miles. Cross the bridge and, 50 yards further along, there is a sheltered car park off the road to the left.

To start the walk, cross the road to the stream and turn left to follow it upstream. Here it is known as Weir Water. Later, after being joined by Chalk Water it becomes Oare Water and, when Badgworthy Water joins it at Malmsmead, it becomes the East Lyn river. Keeping close to the water, there is small brook to be crossed and immediately afterwards a substantial stile to be climbed. Here there is a notice to say that the path to Pittcombe Head is a 'permissive' one and is confirmed with yellow waymarks. After the stile, stay close to the wire fence on the right.

When a large mound appears in front, the path turns left away from the stream to run along the left hand side of the mound. Then it passes through the ruins of long-abandoned cottages and through a small grass enclosure to another small stream. Cross this to enter woodland, turning left and climbing sharply on a worn track which becomes progressively narrower before emerging at the top into an area of oak scrub.

Keep straight on, with a fence to the right until a stile is reached.

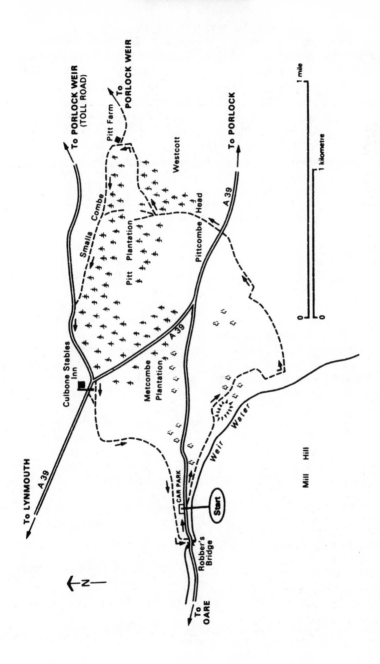

Looking back from here the two hills on the horizon beyond Robber's Bridge are Great Black Hill and Malmsmead Hill. Climb the stile and turn right to follow the fence around the outside of the field. As the high point is reached on the far side of the field, there are splendid views behind of the moorland and reclaimed moorland in the heart of Exmoor.

Still going east-northeast alongside the fence, a steep-sided valley unfolds in front. Turn off left just before meeting the fence above the valley and climb over the high stile. Turn right down a wide track, cross a small stream at the bottom and climb up to follow the fence on the right again. At the end of the fence is yet another stile which emerges straight onto the A39 road immediately opposite Pittcombe Head picnic area. Cross the road and follow the path signposted to Porlock Weir, still yellow waymarked to confirm the route. Soon after the picnic site there is a large gate to go through and then the path is a descent on a wide grassy track which becomes bare as the descent quickens.

Fork right to follow the yellow waymarks through an area where extensive forestry operations have taken place to clear fell before replanting. Keep going downhill until the buildings of Pitt Farm are reached. Here the path joins another from Culbone Inn, the next objective.

Turn left away from the farm and on this stretch there should be red waymarks to confirm the route. This starts off as a wide track by the side of the stream to the right and climbs steadily up Smalla Combe with noticeable seepage of surface water making muddy stretches. As another path joins down from the left, cross the stream to follow it on the opposite bank through a damp stretch. As dry ground is regained the steady climb continues with no undue severity. The drop down to the stream appears to become deeper and deeper until it comes to a dead end as the path reaches the metalled road which runs from Culbone Stables to Porlock Weir. Turn left on this road which runs between stunted pines to the inn. Just before reaching a cattle grid, there is an opportunity to visit an ancient Standing Stone – the 'Culbone Stone' which stands amongst the pines on the right. This will involve a diversion of about 10 minutes.

Go straight across the A39 road and take the path running to the left and behind the inn, signposted to Oareford. This is joined by another path starting from the inn car park and proceeds steadily downhill as a wide track between mixed trees at first, then crossing a dry gully to the open hillside overlooking Metcombe to the left.

Very soon it is possible to see the early part of the walk beside Weir Water and now the path is so cleverly contoured that it seems impossible to descend to Robber's Bridge without a last minute precipitous drop! On reaching the car park it is possible to drive back to the A39 in an easterly direction, away from Oare. However be warned that this road is narrow and steep, with two sharp bends on the steepest part – a miniature Porlock Hill!

Oare Church via Badgworthy Water
3 miles (5 km)

OS sheets 180 and 181
Start: Malmsmead car park, OS map ref. 793478

The next 'Doone Country' walk starts from the centre of Malmsmead which means that there will be more people in evidence than on most of the recommended walks. Malmsmead has become a very popular venue for all those who wish to sample the atmosphere created in the novel Lorna Doone and later on television. The main building in the village is the greatly extended Lorna Doone Farm on the banks of Badgworthy Water. From all accounts, R. D. Blackmore could well have based Plovers' Barrow farm on the one which originally stood here. Badgworthy Water leads back to the 'water slide' at Lank Combe and Hoccombe Water with the ruined cottages of Badgworthy Settlement which resembles the Doone Valley described in the book.

To reach Malmsmead is a minor adventure in itself with steep and narrow picturesque roads to be traversed. Turn off the A39 Porlock to Lynmouth road at either the turning to Brendon or the one near County Gate and follow the signs to Malmsmead. Alternatively, turn off the B3223 Simonsbath to Lynmouth road at Brendon Manor Farm and follow the Brendon Valley road through Rockford and Brendon. Park the car in the picnic area car park.

Leave the car park by the exit adjacent to the toilets and walk past Lorna Doone Farm. Turn left onto the Oare road and cross the bridge over Badgworthy Water. 150 yards further on turn right onto the entrance road to Cloud Farm which is also a public footpath. This passes through fields and a small wood before running alongside the water. As it crosses another cattle grid and climbs towards the farm, heather topped Malmsmead Hill can be seen across to the right, and then further on Great Black Hill.

On reaching Cloud Farm, turn sharp left uphill on the yellow way-marked path signposted to Oare Church. This passes through an open-sided shed and then climbs back up the side of the hill above the drive which has just been walked. The wide dusty or muddy track passes through sheep pens and then, after a gateway, veers off slightly right to follow vehicle tracks which go through another gate into a small wooded combe. Down to the left can be seen the valley of

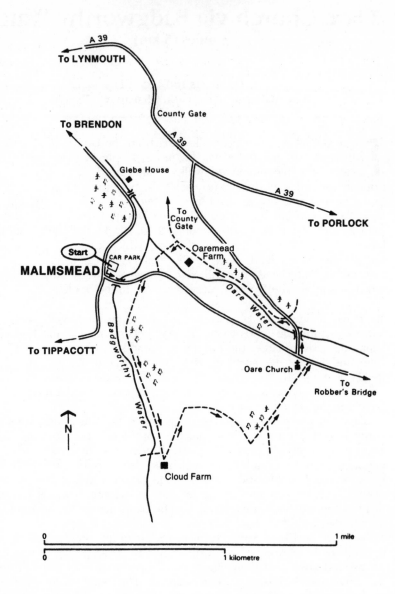

To LYNMOUTH
A 39

County Gate

To BRENDON
A 39

Glebe House

To County Gate

A 39

To PORLOCK

Start
CAR PARK
MALMSMEAD

Oaremead Farm

Oare Water

To TIPPACOTT

Badgworthy Water

Oare Church

To Robber's Bridge

N

Cloud Farm

0 — 1 mile

0 — 1 kilometre

Oare Water with Oare House Allotment topped by the busy A39 on the other side.

Turn left on the other side of the combe to follow the track along the edge of the trees. Go through the wooden gate into the next field and then follow the hedge on the left to the bottom of the field. Do not go through the gate immediately in front but turn right and go through the next gate about 40 yards along. Carry on down the side of the hedge to the road and the first glimpse is obtained of Oare Church tower. On reaching the road turn left and take the opportunity of joining the 30,000 visitors per year who look round this very well maintained little church.

Oare is a very ancient settlement which is mentioned in the Domesday Book and the parish church has been here for over 800 years. It is evident that R. D. Blackmore built some of the characters in his novel on his personal knowledge of the people who used it in his time. His grandfather was the rector of Oare at the beginning of the 19th century. There is no obvious 'cashing in' on the Lorna Doone legend and the visitor's attention is only discreetly drawn to the possible mechanics of the shooting scene described at the end of the novel.

On leaving the church take the Lynmouth road and cross the bridge over Oare Water. Nearly 100 yards after the bridge, turn left through wooden gates to follow a path signposted to Malmsmead. In the first field are two enormous beech trees which show signs of the batterings they have received, even in this sheltered Exmoor valley. The path then passes through a plantation of spruce with water just below to the left. Next in front in Oaremead Farm and the path passes to the right, following a line of power cables.

At the gate turn left towards the water and then turn right along the river bank. Cross the concrete arch bridge and go straight on to pass Parsonage Farm on the left. Turn right on reaching the road, and after passing the Natural History Centre you will soon be back at the Cloud Farm entrance. Return to the car park over the bridge and past Lorna Doone Farm.

The Foreland
2½ miles (4 km)

OS sheet 180
Start: Barna Barrow car park, Countisbury, OS map ref. 753496

A lthough this is only a relatively short walk, it is not recommended for anyone a bit short of wind because the penultimate stage is a steady climb of about 800 feet in ¾ mile up from the lighthouse. However, for anyone else it is well worth while for the views from the top of Countisbury Common, 1000 feet above Lynmouth Bay. If an aversion to heights is suffered, there is an alternative route at Butter Hill which still provides the views without the possible discomfort of slight vertigo.

The start point is in the Exmoor National Park car park on the north side of the A39 road from Lynmouth to Porlock at a point midway between Countisbury village and the private road to the Foreland lighthouse.

Before starting off on the walk, there is a good opportunity of looking at the surrounding area from the car park. Westwards is the town of Lynton with Hollerday Hill behind it to the right. This town was established as a holiday resort about the time of the Napoleonic Wars when it was necessary to create alternatives for those who were accustomed to travel abroad for their holidays. It's fame as the centre for north Devon beauty is now world-wide and, together with Lynmouth, it attracts visitors in increasing numbers all the year round. Over to the left can be seen the two wooded valleys of Farley Water and Hoar Oak Water joining together and then drawing closer to join the larger valley of the East Lyn at Watersmeet. Beyond these can be seen the high ground of the Chains, from where all these rivers except the East Lyn draw their copious supplies of water.

Start the walk by leaving the car park through the gate facing out to sea and then turn left over short cropped grass to follow the wall on the left. It will be noted that the land here belongs to the National Trust, as does much of this beautiful coast line of north Devon. Soon, over the wall to the left can be seen the small village of Countisbury with its weatherbeaten church. Then, in front is the first view of Lynmouth harbour with the cliff railway descending nearly vertically from Lynton. Originally this harbour was the base for the fishing fleet which caught large quantities of herring in the Bristol Channel, but these vanished 300

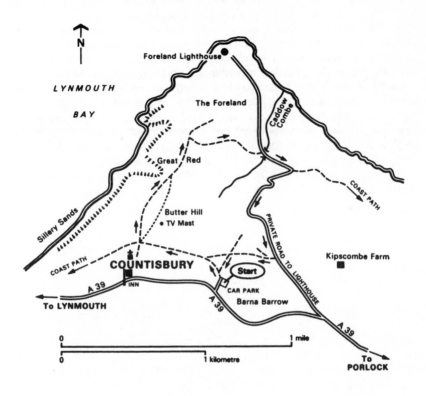

years ago. Later lime and coal was landed here and one of the lime kilns is still preserved on the esplanade.

As the path joins the coast path, there is a well placed seat and a four-way signpost. Turn right here to follow the coast path round Butter Hill above Sillery Sands 800 feet below. This path is wide and very safe but if it is preferred to walk a little further away from the cliffs, turn a little more to the right up to the triangulation point and television relay mast. From here carry straight on down to rejoin the coast path at Great Red where there is protective fencing around a precipitous cliff. Keep straight on past another seat and at the next signpost turn off right and follow the signs to the lighthouse road along the side of a rocky valley.

On reaching the road, if it is wished to take the opportunity of visiting the Foreland lighthouse turn left and follow the road for about 800 yards. To continue this walk, turn right on the road, cross the bridge and commence the long uphill pull. Turn sharp right on the road to leave the coast path, then sharp left and right again.

At this point, looking eastwards up the coast is the aptly named Desolate Farm and behind this can be seen Old Barrow Hill. Here in AD50 the Romans built a small fort where a garrison of about 80 men kept an eye on the troublesome Silures who lived in South Wales.

Continue to climb up the road as it turns sharp left again. 400 yards after this sharp bend, with Kipscombe Hill on the left, turn right onto a wide track which has been roughly asphalted for the first few yards. Take the left fork after about 30 yards and in front an early sight of the television relay mast on top of Countisbury Common confirms the route. Turn left onto the next path which crosses the track and this soon joins another track which ends at the gate of the car park where the walk started.

To the 'Doone Valley'
7½ miles (12 km)

OS sheet 180
Start: Dry Bridge car park, Brendon Common, OS map ref. 759453

A walking programme in Exmoor would not be complete without a visit to the legendary 'Doone Valley'. It is alleged that nine out of ten visitors have previous knowledge of at least two places in Exmoor and these are Tarr Steps and the Doone Valley. A visit to the first is easily accomplished by car, but whichever way the second objective is attained, it must involve a walk of at least four miles. The quick way is to walk up Badgworthy Water and return the same way but the longer route described here is a much more satisfactory achievement and it is not hard going. However it would be best to pick a dry day with good visibility and, if there is a nip in the air, wear an extra jersey for the Brendon Common crossings.

The starting point is on the B3223 road between Simonsbath and Lynton. From Lynton, leave the A39 at Hillsford Bridge and follow the road onto Brendon Common. One mile after crossing the cattle grid onto the open common, pull into the large car park on the left. Just in case the mileometer is not working, this quarried out car park is the second one on the left. From Simonsbath the car park is the first quarried out one on the right about 1½ miles after crossing the cattle grid at Brendon Two Gates.

Walk 50 yards alongside the road towards Simonsbath to a signpost indicating the path to Brendon, Malmsmead and Doone Valley. Turn left to follow this across the open common. On the right hand side of the path is an iron 'Star of Bethlehem' sign which marks the site of a tumulus. During the last war this method of identification was used on open moorland to prevent the destruction of tumuli by tracked vehicles training in the area. Keep straight on where the path forks off left to Brendon and over to the right is the start of Lank Combe, which is crossed twice during this walk.

At the next path junction turn right to descend into the combe. Cross the water and climb up the stony track on the other side to Withycombe Ridge. The path then takes a line parallel with the combe through dense ferns. When these finish on the right, look out for a path which forks slightly right to cross a boggy stretch. This leads to a gate in the bound-

91

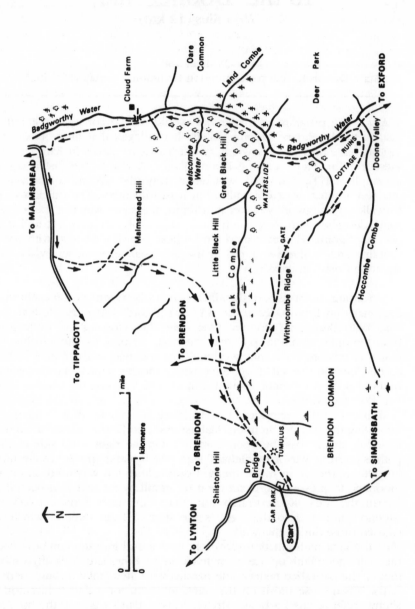

ary wall of the common. If this fork is missed, do not worry unduly but fork off later on and, as long as the combe is left behind, the gate in the wall will be found. Go through this, taking special care to ensure that the gate is secure, because great inconvenience can be caused by the encroachment of commoners' stock onto the privately owned land and vice versa.

To the right now are the combes of Hoccombe and Hoccombe Water on their way down to Badgworthy Water in front. Carry straight on steadily downhill crossing the small stream running down from Withycombe Ridge. It can be seen that the bracken in this area is regularly cut for bedding. This is necessary because straw is not produced in the Exmoor region and must be expensively imported from as far away as East Anglia.

Now the path passes through an old gateway in a row of trees, and this can be considered the start of the Doone Valley, or Hoccombe Combe as it is shown on the map. There is plentiful evidence here of an old settlement, in the form of overgrown field boundaries and ruins of cottages. It is easy to appreciate the attraction of this valley as a place to live, because it is sheltered from all directions and has water, and fuel in the form of wood and peat is readily available. Walk on down past the ruins and turn left towards Malmsmead before reaching the water.

Now the path follows Badgworthy Water and becomes more popular the nearer it gets to Malmsmead. In front is Great Black Hill behind the oaks of Lank Combe, and over on the other side of the water is the Deer Park. The path threads its way through the rocks of Withycombe Ridge Water (keep over to the right for the easiest way through). Then it enters dense trees and rhododendrons before the bridge over Lank Combe.

If a closer view of the 'Water Slide' is required, turn left for about 20 yards after the bridge. After heavy rain this is quite an impressive sight but it was not the location used for the latest television series of Lorna Doone.

The path carries on through more woodland opposite Deer Park Plantation and Land Combe on the other side of the water. Go through the gate at Yealscombe Water, and again take care to see it is closed afterwards. The large barrier across the water at this point is to allow water to pass freely but stop animals getting upstream. Still more woodland and then an open level stretch below Malmsmead Hill. This is the site of the Richard Doddridge Blackmore memorial stone which was placed here in 1969. What a pity that vandals have chosen to record their own visit to this beauty spot in such a selfish manner.

The next landmark is the new bridge across to Cloud Farm. Just upstream from this bridge can be seen the site of the previous bridge which was destroyed in 1952. Now the path forks left, away from the river, to go through a gate into a sunken path with a hedge on the right. Not a very pleasant path, but it doesn't last long! After a dump eyesore on the right the path crosses a stream and climbs to join a metalled road. Turn sharp left to follow this road uphill. It climbs steadily upwards with a good view across to Malmsmead Hill on the left.

Cross the cattle grid, pass under the power cables and keep on to the brow of the hill. Here there is a distinct, gravel surfaced track going off at right-angles to the left. Follow this as it goes in a roughly southerly direction to the right of Malmsmead Hill, and stick to the main track which descends into a shallow combe. Cross the combe and then follow the signposted path to Brendon Common, climbing at first and then sweeping right to rejoin the original path where the right turn was made to cross Lank Combe. From here carry straight on to retrace the early part of the walk past the tumulus.

Hoar Oak Valley and Exe Head
4½ miles (7 km)

OS sheet 180
Start: Brendon Two Gates, OS map ref. 765433

O n Walk 14, the western end of the Chains was visited. This walk penetrates the same area from the east to provide a fairly easy route over the loneliest part of Exmoor. Generally, rights of way are sparse but adequate in the central moorlands and it is just as well to stick to them because although there are no 'bottomless pits', some inconvenience can be experienced if short cuts are attempted. During the course of this walk there are four stream crossings and boggy ground near Blackpits. Ordinary walking boots would be quite satisfactory except during prolonged wet weather when the area is best avoided.

The start point is on the B3223 road from Simonsbath to Lynton at the cattle grid 2½ miles north of Simonsbath. Park on the wide firm verges either side of the road south of the grid.

This place, Brendon Two Gates, gets its name from the special arrangement of gates that were in place here. Two gates were so arranged that whichever way the wind blew, at least one barred animals from leaving or entering the Royal Forest. The word forest did not refer to an area of trees or woodland but was descriptive of a hunting reservation. In fact there were very few trees in the middle of Exmoor until the 19th century. Looking north from the cattle grid onto the open common, one of the first objects to catch the eye is the stone monument on a high point half right. This is a memorial to Colonel R. H. Maclaren, OBE, MC who gave his life to save others when an experimental weapon misfired on this spot in 1941.

To start the walk, go through the cattle grid onto the common and turn left (westward) to follow the stone wall which marks the northern boundary of the old Royal Forest of Exmoor, which is also the boundary between Devon and Somerset. During this part of the walk it is interesting to compare the vegetation on the two sides of the wall. On the common it is typical moorland with heathers, ferns and reeds, but inside the wall molinia grass predominates. This change has been brought about by extensive summer sheep grazing within the Royal Forest boundaries over hundreds of years. It was the principal source of income when the area was reserved for hunting.

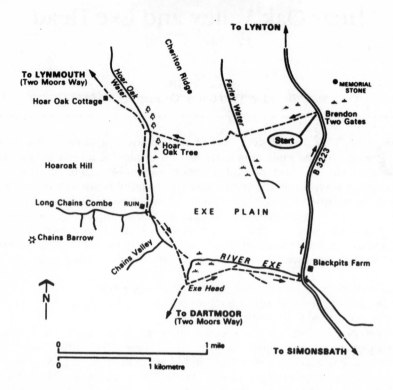

The path descends into the steep-sided combe of Farley Water and the best way up the other side is to tack off up to the right and then bear left again to continue following the wall. As the descent into the next combe is started, over to the right can be seen Hoar Oak Cottage. Until the 1950s this was a shepherd's home but since the acquisition of the land by Exmoor National Park it has been relegated to a shelter for animals. In front is Hoar Oak Hill and half left can be seen the triangulation point on top of Chains Barrow.

Continue to follow the wall down but just before reaching Hoar Oak Water at the bottom turn left through a hunting gate in the wall. Immediately in front, surrounded by railings is the Hoar Oak tree. This is an ancient boundary mark of the Royal Forest and is the latest in a series of oak trees grown here. Although it was planted over sixty years ago in 1916, its progress in this high exposed situation has been very slow and has not been helped in recent years by the erosion of the surround caused by cattle rubbing.

Carry on down to the water, cross it and climb up the track inside the fence to the right. On reaching the two gates at the top, do not go through either of them but turn sharp left to follow the path along the side of the valley. This section of path is narrow but well used by walking connoisseurs and is part of the Two Moors Way between Ivybridge in Dartmoor and Lynmouth in Exmoor. The path climbs very gradually and, after passing under the ruins of another long-abandoned cottage, the wild and rugged Long Chains Combe can be seen up to the right.

Cross the stream running out of this combe and then cross Hoar Oak Water. Now the gradient becomes steeper as the path climbs up to the source of this stream, passing the gash of the Chains Valley on the right. On reaching the open Exe Plain, fork right off the hard track and make for a prominent bank about 20 yards away which runs south. Follow this bank up to the gates at Exe Head. Do not try to short cut across Exe Plain to Blackpits farm which can be seen over to the left.

About 50 yards before reaching the fence, fork off left to go through the large gate with a three-way signpost on the other side. This is literally the head of the Exe river, and water collecting here makes its way via Blackpits, Exford and Winsford to the English Channel at Exmouth. In Saxon times Exe Head was an important road junction where pack horse trains met on their old trails which ran to all points of the compass from here.

Turn left at the signpost and follow the wire fence on the left. Over to the right behind Dure Down is rugged Tangs Bottom where many sheep were buried and suffocated during the blizzard of February 1978.

Stay close to the fence until it turns sharply downwards to the left to cross the infant Exe. Fork right here to follow the path alongside the valley and about 200 yards further on take the left fork to follow the lower more prominent path. Go through a hunting gate and then, after negotiating an exceptionally muddy stretch, go through the gate onto the Brendon Two Gate road. Turn left to follow this road all the way back to the car. This is the least interesting part of the walk but the wide verges allow relaxation and it only takes 20 minutes!

The reason for the unusual width of this moorland road is that it is the final stretch of a vital road which was constructed between Coppleham Cross in the Exe Valley and Brendon Two Gates in 1926-33. From the beginning of the century Dulverton Rural District Council had planned to provide a highway which could bring relief to the villages of Winsford, Exford and Simonsbath during bad weather and this became possible in 1926 when the government supplied the necessary funds to create work for the large number of unemployed men.

Hoar Oak Water and the East Lyn
4 miles (6.5 km)

OS sheet 180
Start: Hillsford Bridge, OS map ref. 741478

In August 1952 it was a miserable holiday month in the Exmoor area with rain falling incessantly on the peat bogs of the central high ground known as the Chains. On Friday 15th August this rainfall became even more intense and the streams flowing both north and south became raging torrents. Then, in the evening a natural disaster occurred in the form of a cloudburst which deposited five inches of rain in an hour, making a total rainfall of nine inches in 24 hours. This produced what can only be described as tidal wave, twenty feet and more high which plunged down the rivers at a speed of 20 mph.

The rivers running north off the moor to Lynmouth drop very quickly to the sea and the force of water and massive boulders tearing down the East and West Lyn rivers caused a terrible flood disaster that night with the loss of 34 lives and structural damage sufficient to change the face of Lynmouth for all time.

This walk follows one of the guilty rivers and it will not be difficult to imagine the horror when the cleaves were full of water and debris. The previous Hillsford bridge was washed away that night and was temporarily replaced by a Bailey bridge built by the army. Later this was replaced by the handsome construction to be seen today. The bridge crosses Hoar Oak Water just as the B3223 road from Simonsbath joins the A39 above Lynmouth. To park the car, drive into the Combe Park Hotel entrance gate and use the National Trust car park immediately on the left.

Leave the car park to cross Hillsford Bridge and turn in through the first gate on the left to walk down the side of Hoar Oak Water which was joined by Farley Water on the other side of the bridge. It will be noted that this area is the National Trust owned estate of Watersmeet, and most of the walk is within this estate which was purchased on the initiative of a group of local people who collected the money from 1931 onwards and then handed the estate to the National Trust for safe keeping.

The wide track follows the rapid descent of Hoar Oak Water through mixed woodland. The series of waterfalls amongst the vast boulders are

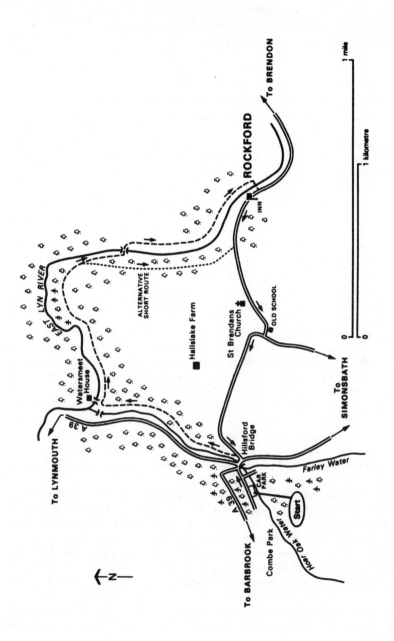

an impressive sight, especially in winter months or after a summer storm up in the moors. As the valley temporarily widens there is a glimpse of open South Hill Common above the steep cleave in front. Then it narrows again and there is a short track down to the left where the most spectacular of the chain of waterfalls can be viewed at close quarters.

As the zigzag path from Watersmeet car park comes down on the other side of the water to cross a bridge below to the left, fork left down steep stone steps to the other end of this bridge. Do not cross it but certainly bide awhile to watch the antics of the dippers who are usually active on the boulders below. Turn right towards Watersmeet House and keeping to this side of the East Lyn river, walk towards Rockford. At the house there is a National Trust shop and a café which must be one of the most beautifully situated of their properties.

The East Lyn does not descend so quickly as Hoar Oak Water and the migratory salmon are able to swim up this river from the sea to spawn in the upper reaches of Oare Water and Badgworthy Water. The ruins of a lime kiln are passed on the left. A little further on, as the path rises to an impressive height above the water, it is possible to look forward up the valley to see traffic travelling along the A39 high above, opposite Barna Barrow. Then there is a seat on the right with a magnificent view through the trees of Myrtleberry Cleave. Just after this seat there is a choice of paths to Rockford. Keep straight on at this point, unless it is wished to slightly shorten the walk (see map for alternative route).

Now the path descends through an area of dense young woodland with a good mixture of hardwoods and conifers. As it comes to the river again, there is the tranquil Horners Pool down to the left, where the river has taken a devious route around a rocky outcrop. This is one of the many named pools where the fishermen try to outwit the wily salmon and trout.

A little further on, cross the bridge and then turn right to follow the river upstream again. There is a stretch of open hillside now for the first time since leaving Hillsford Bridge, and near the top of this climb there is a well positioned seat with a view back down the valley. Back into woods again and here the trees are predominantly handsome straight oaks. At the next seat the path is nearly at water level and the river is running through a rocky channel between peaceful pools where large numbers of trout can normally be seen in the clear water.

Now the first buildings of Rockford appear on the opposite bank. The origin of the place name is obvious from the condition of the river here as it widens out to find a way round large polished rocks. Do not cross the ford but take the path between the river and Rockford Lodge to the bridge. Cross the bridge and then turn right to walk along the road through the village with its inn. There is a steep climb up the road, passing cottages on the right set in beautiful positions above the river with magnificent displays of rhododendrons in their sheltered gardens.

At the top of this hill there is a short breather where the 'short cut' to Rockford joins the road. Keep straight on up the road on a steeper hill with the church tower in front as a target. This is St Brendans Church, the parish church for Brendon which is about 1½ miles away on the other side of Rockford. It was built here in 1738 to replace another church which was the other side of Farley Water, three miles from the village. Some of the stone was removed from the old church together with the sundial which can be seen over the porch.

As the road turns to the right with the worst of the climb over, it passes the old school on the left. At the next T-junction, turn right to follow an unsignposted road which leads all the way back to the start point at Hillsford Bridge. Just before the entrance to Hallslake Farm on the right there are extensive views of Butter Hill and Kipscombe Hill beyond the East Lyn valley, with the farm in the foreground. Further to the left are the ancient earthworks of Wind Hill which lies South of Countisbury Hill. After the farm entrance, there is a steep descent to the bridge, but there is very little chance of encountering any vehicles along this road.

The Valley of Rocks and Lee Valley
5 or 2½ miles (8 or 4 km)

OS sheet 180
Start: Valley of Rocks, Lynton, OS map ref. 710497, or Lee Bay,
OS map ref. 695492

The Valley of Rocks, west of Lynton is one of those places that must be seen to be believed. Somehow, photographs never seem to capture the unusual atmosphere created by the weird rock formation and steep cleaves. It is believed that this was not always a dry valley and thousands of years ago when the sea level was much higher, this could well have been part of the original exit to the sea of the East Lyn river. The precarious looking rock formations have been chiselled out by countless years of weathering action on the mixture of sandstones which make up the rock strata. The veins of softer stone have been eroded, leaving the layers of more resilient stone.

If the shorter walk is selected, drive through the Valley of Rocks, past Lee Abbey and down to the car park above Lee Bay, but if the longer distance is chosen, park in the Exmoor National Park picnic area on the left hand side of the road just before the cricket ground in the Valley. In either case the walks can be conveniently shortened by a mile at a later stage. The directions start from the car park for the longer distance.

Turn left out of the car park to pass the public conveniences on the left. Take the footpath on the right hand side of the road which passes the cricket field, a café and the public car park. Up above to the right is the rock formation known as Rugged Jack. Then there is a gap in the rocks where the cliff path from Lynton enters the valley before Castle Rock which is the very prominent outcrop in front. Look out for the herd of wild goats which are usually to be seen in this area. Years of contact with thousands of visitors have made them very placid, and their welfare is now the responsibility of Lynton Council.

Carry on along the road, and over to the left are the rocks known as the Devil's Cheesering and Mother Meldrum's cave. This lady was the legendary seer who was visited by John Ridd in R. D. Blackmore's Lorna Doone. About 50 yards after the signpost to the cave, fork right onto a path running above. Wringcliffe Bay down to the right. This path ends at a wall, turn left here to follow a path running alongside this wall back up to the road again, joining it at the Toll Lodge.

Follow the road again, using the wide grass verge on the left hand side

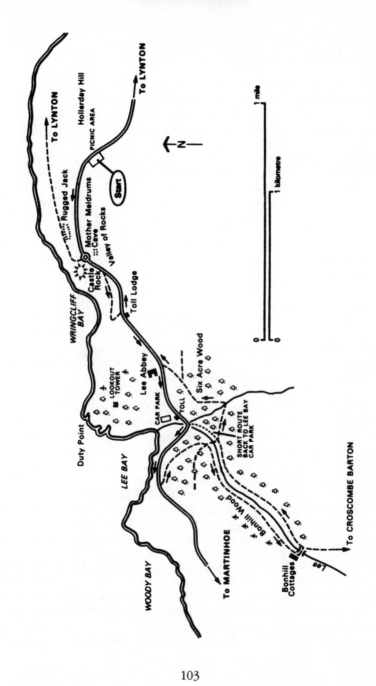

to make for safer walking, although there is normally little traffic to worry about along here. On the right is Lee Abbey Farm and then Lee Abbey itself. Now there is a descent to the toll gate with Lee Bay down to the right.

This is the starting point for those taking the shorter walk.

Keep to the road passing Lee Cottage on the right and climbing up above the bay. Looking across to the right, there is the lookout tower in Cuddycleave Wood above Duty Point. As the road emerges into the open there is a perfect view of Woody Bay in front.

At this point turn sharp left off the road to follow a path signposted as a bridleway to Croscombe Barton. This passes through the dense Bonhill Wood, the gradient decreases and there is evidence of active woodland management where replanting has taken place. Along here it is possible to shorten the walk by a mile if the signposted route for the Woodland Walk to Lee Abbey is followed. Carry straight on for the planned walk and soon there are narrow lush meadows down to the left. Then Bonhill Cottages can be seen in front.

Turn sharp left over the bridge in front of these cottages and then, at the top of a short climb, fork left to climb over a stile to follow the foot-path signposted to Lee Abbey. This is a very different kind of path and care is needed over the first 200 yards or so. Just after the stile there is a tile covered building. Pass to the left of this and then turn sharp right at the end of the shed to climb up some rock steps. Then the path descends to cross a small stream with a short steep ascent over rocks on the other side. From here the path is a narrower grassy strip through wild wood-land and it runs parallel with the track previously followed on the other side of the stream. Be prepared to clamber over or round the occasional fallen tree along this path. Fork left downhill on the occasion where there is a choice of paths and as the path descends nearly to water level, it passes a wide vehicular bridge and is then rejoined by the yellow way-marked Woodland Walk as it crosses the Lee on a foot bridge.

If the car is parked at Lee Bay car park, fork left a few yards after this junction onto a signposted footpath. This follows the Lee and emerges onto the road just by Lee Cottage. Otherwise carry straight on and very soon Lee Abbey can be seen through the trees. The track swings right and then turns left over a bridge near the head of a combe. Just above this to the right there is a fine stand of mature beeches and then there are the occasional chestnut and ash to make a change from the predominantly oak woodland.

When the path forks, take the left fork to Lee Abbey and in a few yards Lee Bay can be seen down below. As the path leaves the woods it rejoins the toll road opposite the entrance to Lee Abbey. Turn right to retrace the early part of the walk back to the picnic area car park.

Heddon Mouth
2 miles (3 km)

OS sheet 180
Start: Hunter's Inn, OS map ref. 655480

On Exmoor it is very difficult to plan a circular walk without an appreciable gradient at some stage, and, on looking back through the previous 29 walks, it must be admitted that they all contain at least one significant ascent. This last walk is only a short one of just over two miles, but it is nearly level, is in spectacular surroundings and is on National Trust owned land. These qualities should provide the encouragement to visit the starting point of Hunter's Inn and, after the walk, create the enthusiasm to sample more of the interesting walks which radiate from this centre.

The easiest way of reaching the starting point by car is to travel on the A399 from Blackmore Gate towards Combe Martin for two miles and then turn off right on the turning signposted to Trentishoe and Hunter's Inn. There is an added bonus here in the form of a spectacular journey over the last two miles of this route. It is also possible to leave the A39 just north of the turning to Parracombe but this is a very narrow and steep road which can involve much reversing! At Hunter's Inn there is the hotel itself with a very wide range of facilities, shops and public toilets. The car park is opposite the toilets.

To start the walk, go down the road towards the inn. Around here there are sure to be exotic peacocks who treat the vicinity of the inn as if it has been their home for many years. Fork right just before the front of the inn and then take the wide footpath immediately in front. Go through the gate and then fork left for the path to Heddons Mouth Beach. Down to the left are the well kept gardens of the hotel which are usually open to visitors. After the gardens, the path follows the Heddon River. In summertime the river is nearly concealed by massive clumps of Japanese knot weed which has become established here in the last few years.

As the path starts to rise in Road Wood there is a choice of paths. Either stay on the wide hard surfaced path which goes through the oaks at a higher level or take the narrower lower path near the river bank which can be damp in places. The paths rejoin where there is a bridge which carries the coast path over the river and, as open ground is

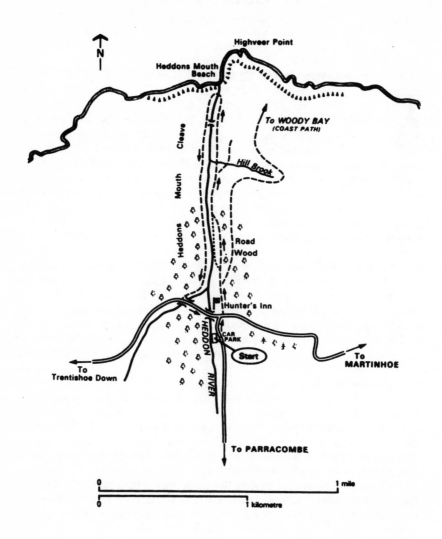

reached, there is a startling view of Heddons Mouth Cleave on the other side of the river. This rises nearly vertically to a height of 700 feet. As the path gets nearer to the mouth of the river it will be noticed that the trees become more and more stunted as they become more exposed to the wind from the sea. Keep straight on where the coast path to Woody Bay forks off to the right.

Hill Brook is crossed and up above to the right can be seen a path making its way along the side of the steep valley down which this brook descends. This path follows the route of an old carriage road which ran from Hunter's Inn to Woody Bay, past the site of an old Roman signalling station, and nearly 700 feet above the jagged rocks between Highveer Point and Wringapeak. It must have been quite a nerve-wracking experience riding on top of a carriage along this road!

As the bridge across the river is approached, the rocky shambles of Highveer Point can be seen to the right. Unless the river is running high, it is not necessary to cross the bridge. Carry straight on and cross by the stepping stones above the beach. With care it is possible to swim from this beach and years ago it was used for landing cargo from coasters. Limestone which was landed here was burnt in the lime kiln on the edge of the beach, and the remains of this kiln can be examined after crossing the river. Lime is essential to sweeten the predominantly acid ground on Exmoor and, before the present road system was constructed, it was always more convenient to bring in the limestone and fuel to the nearest landing point on the coast.

The path now returns on the west side of the river, climbing slightly and then returning to the river bank level at the bridge. After passing through an open area there is a well-built dry stone wall on the left which separates the scree from the mixed woodlands of water-loving trees including among others ash and alder together with sycamore, beech, birch, and elder.

As it enters an ash wood the path becomes nearly enclosed for a short stretch by a hedge on the left above verdant meadows. This is replaced by a stone wall and now there are a lot of hartstongue on both sides of the path.

As the hotel comes into sight, the path veers off to the right and after passing a memorial garden 'Harry's Orchard' on the left goes through a gate onto the Trentishoe road. Turn sharp left to follow the road over two bridges back to Hunter's Inn and the car park.